MOSAIC

JEWISH
LIFE
IN
FLORIDA

A DOCUMENTARY EXHIBIT FROM 1763 TO THE PRESENT

Dr. Henry Alan Green
Associate Professor of Sociology & Religion
University of Miami

Marcia Kerstein Zerivitz
Community Consultant

DEDICATION

Dedicated to the Florida pioneers
who shaped the Jewish communities
in which we live today.

FIRST EDITION
Library of Congress Catalog Card Number: 90-92231
Printed in the United States of America

ISBN 1-879438-00-3

Credits
Rachel Heimovics, Editorial Consultant
Vanessa S. Allen, Designer
Bob Greenberg, Artifact Photography
Karen Tina Sheskin, Typography
Printed by Hallmark Press, Miami, Florida

Cover
Felix Glickstein on alligator in Jacksonville, Florida, 1916.

TABLE OF CONTENTS

LETTER FROM
DR. JACOB MARCUS

In all probability there were Jews in Florida as early as the sixteenth century. When Columbus sighted land in 1492 the very first person over the side--so it would seem--was Luis de Torres, the interpreter, a born Jew. I have no doubt that among the early Spanish settlers in Florida there were some Marranos, crypto-Jews, who hoped to elude the Inquisition. However, no identification has yet been made of these secret Jews in this New World colony. What is beyond question, however, is that the archives disclose that as early as the second decade of the nineteenth century Jewish entrepreneurs invested heavily in Florida lands. One speculator bought well over a hundred and fifty thousand acres for this purchase.

In the 1840s David Levy Yulee, a born Jew, went to Congress and later to the Senate; he was the first Florida congressman.

No permanent Jewish community institutions developed in the state until the third quarter of the century. Among the pioneers were immigrants who established synagogues in Jacksonville and in Pensacola. It was not until the first decades of the twentieth century that Jewish life began to take on flesh in southern Florida. To be sure, no one in those days ever dreamt that there would be a mass influx into that part of the state after World War II. Today the south Florida region shelters the third largest Jewish community in America, after New York and Los Angeles.

David Levy Yulee's father, Moses Elias Levy, was a devoted Jew. He acquired large holdings in Florida as early as 1818 and even dreamt of establishing a Jewish colony there. More important was his determination to create a nationwide ''Institution'' that would launch a Jewish cultural revolution. This visionary never reached his goal. Now, at the turn of the twenty-first century, Florida is challenged to bring to birth a Jewish renaissance commensurate with the numbers. *MOSAIC: Jewish Life in Florida* is a promise that this hope will be fulfilled. There is every reason to believe that by the year 2,000 the state, with 750,000 Jews, will become a hearth of intense Jewish life and scholarship. This is its challenge; this is its opportunity.

Dr. Jacob R. Marcus
Director, American Jewish Arhives

A M E R I C A N   J E W I S H   A R C H I V E S

PREFACE

MOSAIC is a story about people. Each tile represents a Floridian who has shared his or her life. Over a period of five years, thousands of Floridians have opened their hearts. Hundreds have collected oral histories, photographs and artifacts. People from Pensacola to Key West, Tallahassee to Jacksonville, early pioneers and recent refugees, young and old, collectively created the *MOSAIC: Jewish Life in Florida* exhibit.

MOSAIC is an ethnic story. Each tile exposes an immigrant's experience and the building of community. Russian, German, Moroccan, Turk, Cuban, Peruvian, Israeli and Canadian are just a few of the nationalities represented. Culturally they span Hispanic, European, North African, Middle Eastern, and North American life-styles. Their stories are both universal and unique. Forming a family and making a living are not dependent on religion, gender or class.

MOSAIC is a Jewish story. Each tile is a window into Jewish life. Beginning with the Spanish conquest of Florida in the sixteenth century, the saga of Florida Jewry is spun. Asking an age-old question, "How do Jews balance the preservation of ethnic identity with the pressures to acculturate," the exhibit provides many answers. The Jewish experience, its lifecycle and seasonal events, has been colored by the tropical Florida sun.

No project of such a dimension would have been possible without a leader. Marcia Kerstein Zerivitz has traveled the state extensively, created community task forces to identify and collect the inventory, listened to stories day and night, and more. She has breathed life into all those she has touched and joined with them in the creation of community. I feel especially blessed to have worked by her side.

I cannot thank enough the countless volunteers. I especially want to express my appreciation to our task force community chairs who have given of themselves so generously: Heléne Herskowitz, Miami; Sylvia Shorstein, Jacksonville; Sandra Angel Malamud, Sarasota; Beverly Kaiman, Pensacola; Nancy Goldberg, Fort Lauderdale; Rabbi Stanley Garfein, Tallahassee; Doris Rosenblatt and Nell Friedman, Tampa; Estelle Kaplan, Brevard County; Helen Weinfeld, Naples; and Elaine Leventhal, Ft. Myers.

I am also very grateful to Andy Brian and the entire staff of the Historical Museum of Southern Florida, who went beyond the call of duty to prepare the exhibit; Laura Hochman of the Soref Jewish Community Center and Abraham Gittelson of the Central Agency for Jewish Education, who from day one were part of the project; Lisa Medin Beriro and Lynn Schulte, who served as Research Assistants; Elliott Zerivitz, Eileen Hirsch, Bonnie Cohn Levy, Shirley Robbins and Lydia Jacobs who were there to lend a helping hand; Robin Rosenbaum of the Ringling School of Art, for her creative MOSAIC poster; the Academic Advisory Board: Judith Elkin, Paul George, Diane Lewis, Ormond Loomis, Abraham Peck, Samuel Proctor, Ira Sheskin, Marshall Sklare and Charlton Tebeau; the late Janet Chusmir and the *Miami Herald*; the American Jewish Archives; the American Jewish Historical Society; the Southern Jewish Historical Society; the Florida Historical Society; Joan Morris and the staff of the Florida State Photographic Archives; the Florida Chapter of the American Sephardic Federation; Sepharad 92 and the University of Miami.

MOSAIC would not have been possible without the support of the Florida Legislature through the Department of State and the Florida Endowment for the Humanities. They believed in MOSAIC from its inception and provided the means to conduct research and fabricate the exhibit.

For me, MOSAIC typifies the soul of Florida. It affirms the best of people, the richness of our multi-cultural heritage and the potential to share dreams. Endorsed by the National Columbus Quincentenary Jubilee Commission, the Columbus Florida Hemispheric Commission and the Israeli and Spanish governments, MOSAIC integrates the past with the present and creates a vision for tomorrow. Historically, it redefines not only the Jewish experience in America, but also the role Jews and Hispanics have played together for centuries in forging trails in Florida's frontier.

There is a midrash (parable) that speaks to Jewish heritage but is universal in its message. An old man, bent with years, toils in the field. He digs the earth, oblivious to those who have stopped to watch him. Slowly and gently he moves a young sapling to the hole he has dug. Carefully placing the tree he stands back and smiles. One of the observers who has watched the old man struggle with his task inquires why he has spent so much energy planting a tree that he will never see grow. The old man replies, "as my father planted for me, so I plant for my children."

It is our goal that the thousands of items that now constitute the Mosaic Floridiana Judaica collection be housed in a permanent Jewish Museum in Florida after the exhibit has traveled. The MOSAIC exhibit and catalog is only the beginning; it is not inclusive. We hope that you will envision with us a permanent repository where Florida's stories can be shared and passed on to future generations.

Henry Alan Green
Director, MOSAIC and Judaic Studies Program,
University of Miami
Erev Pesach 5751/1991

FLORIDA JEWRY: 1763-1990*

MOSAIC: Jewish Life in Florida is the exciting saga of one ethnic group's encounter with a new world. Jews have participated in Florida's growth and have left their footprints across the entire state. MOSAIC explores and documents the meaning of the Jewish experience in Florida in the framework of the American Jewish experience.

The role of ethnicity in American society cannot be overstated.[1] The earliest Puritans in Massachusetts were bonded to a European culture similar to Holocaust survivors living in Florida today. Fleeing persecution three hundred years ago, the Puritans came to America holding fast to "old country" values. Their descendants acculturated. Holocaust survivors, fleeing tragedy, came to America tied to an European ethos. Today, their children and grandchildren are acculturating. Attachment to a foreign people and culture keeps ethnicity alive and impedes the acculturation process.

Jews in America have continually struggled between Americanization and ethnic survival, veering between these strong crosscurrents, often without resolution. Jewish identification may have been muted by modernization, mass education and American culture, but ethnicity remains a factor in self-perception and in the shaping of modern American society. For example, think how twentieth century American culture has been infused by Jewish ethnicity.

Scholars themselves are caught up in the conflicts between assimilation and ethnicity. In the late twentieth century, the criteria for Jewish identity are constantly debated among them. Will Herberg[2] argued in the 1950s that religion has replaced ethnicity as the focus of group identity. Yet Herbert Gans[3] more recently observed that one's identification to an ethnic heritage is no more than symbolic. Steven Cohen's[4] sociological writings of the last decade continually illustrate the changing quality of Jewish identity.

In Florida today there are a wide range of roles and behaviors that foster Jewish identity. Some Jews affiliate with a synagogue, a community center or a Zionist organization. Some read and write Ladino or Yiddish or modern Hebrew. Some seek their identity through Jewish music and art or through family genealogy or through local history projects. Over 750,000 Jews live in Florida, 650,000 between Palm Beach and Miami.[5] For each one, there are countless ways to fulfill the quest for Jewish identity.

Florida was not always the place of choice for Jews. From 1513 to 1763—half of its nearly five centuries of European settlement—Florida was not receptive to those professing Judaism. Those who migrated to Florida after 1763, and until our century, were drawn for many reasons other than finding an existing Jewish community. Florida was neither a Promised Land nor a new Diaspora.

Only since World War II have numbers of Jews moved to Florida to join an existing Jewish community. Like other Sunbelt states, Florida has received an increasing volume of Northerners.[5] Jewish refugees and Jews from South Africa, Arab lands and the Soviet Union have moved into Florida.

Florida's proximity to Latin America and its increasing Hispanic emigration have also been factors in Jewish migration. Jews from these countries immigrated to South Florida to be close to the Hispanic community. Beginning with the post-Castro migration of Cubans, Hispanic Jews have since been joined by Jews from Colombia, Peru, Puerto Rico, Argentina and other Latin countries.

Jewish population density and other demographic statistics are a measure of Jewish identity. The trickle of Jews who migrated to Florida before 1940 accounted for approximately one percent of the state's two million population and less than 1 percent of the United States' five million Jews.[7] Before 1940, Jewish settlers in Florida tended to be more assimilated. Perhaps as ties to traditional Jewish life weakened, they were more willing to move to a Florida without Jews. Or perhaps, once in Florida, it was their isolation from other Jews that hastened their assimilation.

What was life like for Jews in Florida before 1940? Did they forgo aspects of their cultural and religious distinctiveness to integrate? Were those who were more traditional able to practice their rituals and customs, remain communally involved and maintain in-group marriages? Did Jewish identification reflect ethnic bonds and/or a religious commitment? Can one speak of a viable Florida Jewish community prior to World War II?

Florida history and its Spanish origins have suffered from the Anglo-centrism of American historians. So, too, has the story of America's earliest Jews. Textbooks cite the twenty-three Jews who arrived in New Amsterdam in 1654 as the first Jews who came to America. In 1954 American Jewish communities across the breadth of the nation celebrated this tercentenary.[8] But, 150 years before the twenty-three arrived in New Amsterdam, Sephardic Jews were living in the Western Hemisphere. Some New Christians, or secret Jews, sailed with Christopher Columbus in 1492. Victims of the Spanish Inquisition and the Expulsion—which coincided with Columbus' first voyage—they survived by donning Christian masks. Spanish historian Salvador de Madariaga and other scholars speculate that Columbus himself was of Jewish origin.[9]

Jacob Marcus' scholarly analysis of the early American period and Stephen Birmingham's popularized *The Grandees* both acknowledge the role of Sephardic settlers in the mercantile trade in the Americas in the sixteenth and seventeenth centuries.[10]

Spain exported the Inquisition to the Americas, where it began in Mexico in 1528 and soon spread to Colombia and Peru. Legitimated Jewish communities appeared in the Caribbean after Dutch and English conquests allowed Spanish Marranos to emerge openly as Jews: Curacao in 1634, Surinam in 1639 and Jamaica in 1655.[11] Martin Cohen, Cecil Roth and Seymour Liebman have chronicled the secret communities of Jews in the Spanish and Portuguese Americas.[12]

Converted Jews may have come with Ponce de Leon when he landed in Florida in 1513. Research projects, under the direction of the Judaic Studies Program, University of Miami, are exploring the ties between the Spanish Americas (post 1513) and the early New Amsterdam Jewish community founded in 1654. Current data suggest that Pedro Menendez Marqués, the third Spanish Governor of Florida from 1577-1589, may have been a Converso.[13]

The perception that Jews were late arrivals in Florida parallels the belief that ascribes the founding of the United States of America to the Pilgrims on Plymouth Rock. One-half century before the *Mayflower* arrived (1620), the Spanish were claiming sovereignty of the Florida colony of St. Augustine (1565), the oldest continental city in the United States. Just as the British, French and Dutch colonized the northeast United States, the Spanish colonized the southeast. As we approach 1992, the Quincentenary of Columbus' encounter with the New World, the cultural heritage of Americans still lacks a Spanish perspective.

These biases also explain why scholars have not looked to Colonial Florida as a place of settlement for Conversos and Marranos. Few have asked whether the Marranos who came to the Caribbean, Mexico and South America also journeyed to Florida between 1513 and 1654. An ongoing research goal of *MOSAIC: Jewish Life in Florida* is to fill this vacuum in American Jewish history.

Spanish domination of the southern United States extended into the eighteenth century. Spain lost Florida to Britain in the Treaty of Paris in 1763. The French turned over Louisiana to the Spanish by the same treaty and some Jews, who feared Spanish discrimination policies, moved from New Orleans to Pensacola in West Florida.

Joseph de Palacios, Samuel Israel and Alexander Solomons arrived in Pensacola in 1763 and soon bought property and stores just as other Southern whites did. They were joined by others, including Isaac Mendes of Jamaica, who migrated to West Florida in 1763 and to Pensacola in 1766, and Samuel Judah, who moved to Pensacola in 1767.[14] Isaac Monsanto sold family slaves to finance his trip from New Orleans to Pensacola. The Spanish governor expelled Monsanto with these words: "There are to leave this province...before the end of the next month the Jew Monsanto, for the reason that [he is] undesirable on account of the nature of [his] business and of the religion [he] profess[es]."[15]

All these merchants had extensive commercial contacts in the Caribbean trade and in Colonial America. De Palacios, Israel and Solomons supplied wood and other goods to the British and traded with Jews in Charleston, South Carolina, and Savannah, Georgia.[16] Monsanto provisioned the British Commander of West Florida for an expedition up the Mississippi River.[17] Mendes sold goods for use as "Indian presents" to West Florida Governor Johnstone in 1763.[18]

Although Bertram Korn notes that "there were never enough [Jews in British Florida] to form a quorum for religious worship," preserving their Jewish identity was important to some of them.[19] De Palacios moved to Charleston, South Carolina, in 1778, in part to be closer to an established Jewish community.[20] Manuel Arias, the son of a Jewish slave trader, resided in Pensacola, and records show that he fathered a son in 1783.[21] Besides Arias, the Monsanto clan, and a son of de Palacios, Jewish family records in West Florida during the British period are undocumented. The economic frontier shifted frequently, and colonial Jews were constantly on the move. According to Korn, what is remarkable is that "not one anti-Jewish slur appears in any document" of this period in Florida.[22]

In 1783 Florida reverted to Spain. Some Jews fled Florida to the present states of Georgia, South Carolina, New York and Pennsylvania; others migrated to Florida.[23] Several Polish Jewish families owned stores on Charlotte Street in St. Augustine in 1785.[24] Abraham Mordecai was an Indian trader in West Florida during this period.[25] A few resided in Tallahassee. For the most part, these were isolated individuals far from their home communities. Itinerant Jewish traders were linked to the Spanish, English, French and American trade routes.

Religious life for Jews in Colonial Florida between 1763 and 1821 is difficult to trace. Florida's Jewish population was so small that it is unlikely there were any congregations or organizations such as those in New York; Newport, Rhode Island; Philadelphia; and Charleston, South Carolina. There is no correspondence concerning requests for rabbis to come from Europe, and there are no records written in Ladino, Yiddish or Hebrew. Jews in Florida during this period had little access to such traditional aspects of Jewish life-style as kosher food, Jewish schools and Jewish spouses.

In 1821 the American government purchased Florida from Spain for 5 million dollars and Florida became a United States territory. The young nation, envious of Florida's ports and its access to the Caribbean, viewed Florida as strategic to its nineteenth century foreign policy.

Florida is a huge land mass and 1,146 miles of coastline are surrounded on three sides by water— the Caribbean, the Gulf of Mexico and the Atlantic. In the early nineteenth century, Florida was rich in such natural resources as citrus, lumber, and cotton, but it was very inhospitable because of its climate. Mosquitoes and yellow fever epidemics played havoc with the small population. There were few health facilities. Advances stemming from the industrial revolution in Europe and America had little or no impact on Florida.

In the period between the exchange of Florida from Spain to the United States (1819-1821), entrepreneurs capitalized on real estate opportunities. Some in Cuba, a Spanish territory, took advantage of these developments. Moses Levy, a St. Thomas lumber merchant and Cuban businessman, purchased over 50,000 acres in Micanopy, part of the 289,000 acre Arredondo grant.[26]

Levy was a descendent of a Sephardic family, Abenyule, who migrated to Morocco following the 1492 Spanish expulsion.[27] In Morocco the family name was translated Ibn Yulee, and in Gibraltar it was changed to Levy.[28] Moses Levy came to St. Thomas in 1800.[29] He began a successful lumber business with a cousin, Philip Benjamin, the father of Judah P. Benjamin.[30] The partnership did extremely well trading with the United States, Europe and the Cuban government. Levy married Hannah Abendanone in 1803, and they had two sons and two daughters while living in St. Thomas.[31] Levy was a "literalist" Jew who practiced his religion fervently and went out of his way to follow tradition.

Moses Levy moved to Havana in 1816 and contracted with the Spanish government to furnish supplies to the army. In 1821 he moved to Florida. He brought sugar cane and fruit trees for his plantations. He received his certificate of citizenship on March 23, 1822.[32]

Several other Jews were naturalized in St. Augustine at about the same time: George Levy, a planter from London; Lewis Solomon, a watchmaker from London; Levy Rodenberg, a grocery owner from Amsterdam; and Isaac Hendricks, a planter from South Carolina.[33]

In this same year, 1822, Virginia Myers was born to Louisa and Samuel Myers in Pensacola.[34] Michael Lazarus moved from Charleston to Daytona Beach and bought land.[35] The Florida Jewish population in the late 1820s numbered thirty to forty people, far less than 1 percent of the state's population of thirty-five thousand.[36]

When Levy bought his land in Micanopy, Florida, his intent was to establish a Jewish colony as a safe haven for refugee Jewish families. Levy's European travels had made him keenly aware of the contrast between the freedoms enjoyed by American Jews and the hardships of their European brethren. He corresponded with Jewish leaders at Shearith Israel Synagogue in New York and Beth Elohim in Charleston, and with Rebecca Gratz in Philadelphia about his plans for an agricultural colony. Eventually, Levy bought advertisements in the European press to publicize his project. In a letter to Isaac Goldsmid, Moses Levy reveals his skill at conducting a campaign for financial support:

"I call on you as a religious Person...for in helping the fallen House of Israel, [you are] really and truly assisting the human race at large."[37]

Levy called his plantation New Pilgrimage. It

9

resembled a later kibbutz, where everyone worked the land and studied Hebrew. When the first settlers arrived in 1822, water power was generated, and houses, a stable, and a cornhouse were built. By 1841 Levy had spent $18,000 to provide housing, food, clothing and wages for his workers, but the project failed.[38]

Levy added to his holdings by purchasing land from Antonio Fernandez Mier, another Sephardic Jew, who had profited by the territorial agreement between the United States and Spain.[39] By the 1840s Levy owned land on the St. Johns River and on Tampa Bay, in addition to his large holdings in Alachua County. Few Jews came to Levy's plantations. Those who did either died of disease or soon migrated north to more healthful Jewish communities like Charleston or to the growing western Florida economic centers of Pensacola and Tallahassee.

Moses Levy was a premature Zionist who wanted New Pilgrimage to be a homeland for Jews similar to Mordecai Noah's Ararat, in upstate New York. Through his correspondence with Rebecca Gratz about Jewish education, Levy kept abreast of Noah's plans. Stimulated by progress in educational developments from his trips north, he became a proponent for free education in Florida and was a charter officer of the Florida Education Society.[40]

Levy was also an early advocate for the abolition of slavery. John Forester wrote in 1829 that "Mr. Levy has by his conduct and discourses at meetings of Jews and Christians over...his plan for the abolition of Negro slavery, made his name so well known as to render any further introduction of him to public notice unnecessary."[41]

Actively involved in defending Judaism, Levy corresponded with Christians on religious matters. Levy was known in national and international circles, and some of his letters on this topic were published in England by Thomas Thrush in *Letters to the Jews*.[42] Isaac Leeser considered Levy a "professing Jew" and Samuel Myers of Norfolk, Virginia sought out Levy's counsel when organizing a congregation. Dr. Daniel Peixotto of New York's Shearith Israel publicly declared that Moses Levy "deserves the gratitude and love of his brethren."[43]

To insure that his younger son, David, would have a strong Jewish identity, Levy sent him to Norfolk, Virginia in 1819, to receive both a secular and Jewish education.[44] When David returned to Florida in 1827, he worked on his father's plantation. David wished to become a lawyer; Moses Levy disagreed.[45] He believed that after the age of Bar Mitzvah, children should be financially independent.

David left, studied law in St. Augustine, and was admitted to the bar in 1832.

There are no records of synagogues during the Territorial Period 1821 to 1845 or the establishment of any Jewish institutions, yet a trickle of Jews continued to migrate to Florida. Raphael Jacob Moses opened a store in Tallahassee in 1837, became a lawyer in Apalachicola and was a delegate from Florida to the 1847 Democratic National Convention.[46] In 1839 Emanuel Judah, an actor, built a theater in Apalachicola. Colonel Leon Dyer of Baltimore, David Camden de Leon, an army doctor from South Carolina and Samuel Noah, one of the first graduates of West Point, served in the Florida Indian Wars (1835-1842; 1855-1858).[47] Also a West Point graduate, Abraham C. Meyers was an Army Quartermaster during the Indian Wars. As a tribute to his service, Ft. Myers was named for him by his father-in-law, General David E. Twiggs, the fort commander.[48]

During the 1840s more and more immigrants poured into the United States from central Europe, especially from the German states. German speaking Jews began to ripple into Florida as opportunities arose. When Florida became a state on March 3, 1845, fewer than one hundred Jews lived among its 66,500 people.[49] Most lived in the northern part of the state, where they engaged in the mercantile trade.

David Levy was instrumental in establishing Florida as the twenty-seventh state through his roles as landowner, lawyer and segregationist. As a territorial delegate from 1841 to 1845, Levy eloquently persuaded Floridians of the advantages of land grants if they joined the Union. In 1845, the year of statehood, David Levy applied to the legislature to reclaim the Yulee family name. In that pivotal year, David Levy Yulee became one of Florida's United States senators. He was the first known Jew to serve in the United States Senate, arriving there seven years before his cousin Judah P. Benjamin was elected from Louisiana. Throughout Levy's political career he represented the views of the white, Southern agricultural plantation system, first against the Seminole Indians and later against the Union.

Yulee married Nancy Wickliffe, the daughter of a former Kentucky governor who was a member of President Tyler's cabinet. Although their children were reared as Christians, there is no evidence that Yulee ever converted.[50] Nor is there evidence that he was ever victimized by anti-Semitism in Florida; but John Quincy Adams, in the early 1840s, referred to Levy as "the Jew Delegate from Florida."[51]

During the Antebellum Period, David Levy Yulee

David Levy Yulee
Son of Moses Levy. Helped draft Florida's constitution
and elected first U.S. Senator from Florida in 1845.
Organized The Florida Railroad Company in 1853.
Yulee Park in Homosassa Springs and Levy County
honor his family.

took a break from serving in Washington between 1851 and 1855 to build a railroad from Fernandina to Cedar Key, the first rail line to cross the state from the Atlantic to the Gulf. The railway was designed to transfer freight from the flourishing European trade to destinations bordering the Gulf of Mexico. Not only was it economically appealing to shippers and merchants but it was also a safer route. The Florida reef's toll on shipping was staggering. Through this effort, Yulee and his Democratic friends brought large amounts of capital into Florida and developed a cross-state telegraph line and a fast-mail ship route from Cedar Key on the Gulf Coast to Havana.

Steamships sailed from New York to Savannah, then to Jacksonville on the St. Johns River and on to Palatka and Sanford. Retail stores grew in number as did tourist boarding homes as people began to realize the attractions of life in the interior. Fernandina, on the Atlantic Coast, became an emporium of commerce.

Immigrants from Prussia, Bavaria, Bohemia, and Austria straggled into northern towns in the aftermath of the European revolutions of 1848. In 1849 Samuel Fleischman came to Marianna.[52] Philip Dzialynski from Prussia reached Jacksonville in 1850, bringing his father and eight siblings.[53] In the 1850s the Gundersheimers, Forcheimers and Dannheissers came to Pensacola, and Robert Williams arrived in Tallahassee.[54] Just prior to the Civil War the Solomons, Benjamins and Foxes migrated to Ocala.[55]

The first recorded Jewish community institution was established in Jacksonville in 1857. When six Jews died of yellow fever, the Jacksonville Hebrew cemetery was founded.[56] Jewish holidays and life-cycle events were occasions for the few families to get together in their homes to maintain ethnic and religious identity.

When Philip Dzialynski married Ida Ehrlich in 1856, Jews from Jacksonville and nearby communities assembled to celebrate. They reassembled the following year when George was born.[57]

With the exception of Key West, which was always a refuge for pirates and a mercantile center for trade with the Caribbean, there was no growth in Florida south of Orlando. The discomfort from insects and weather kept settlers away.

Florida was on an economic roller coaster. Each boom was quickly followed by recession or depression. The hopes and investments of capitalists, especially in the cotton industry, were increasingly volatile.

Meanwhile the debate over abolition became more polarized. By 1860 the United States had moved into conflict between those who wanted a country based on a Southern agrarian slave-holding economy and those who favored industrialization and abolition. Sharply different traditions and values further exasperated the division. David Levy Yulee, reelected Senator in 1855, gave outspoken support to the Southern ideology of state's rights and slavery.[58] In 1861 Yulee moved for secession and within months the Civil War commenced.[59] The next year he left on the last train from Fernandina on March 3 as Union forces approached. Although an advocate of Southern Democratic interests, Yulee held no official political position from 1862 to 1865. His sugar plantation at Homosassa was a shelter for blockade runners.[60]

During the Civil War most Florida Jews perceived themselves as Southerners and supported the Confederacy. Slavery was not viewed as a moral issue but an issue of state's rights. Michael Levy of Pensacola, William Fox of Ocala, Morris Dzialynski and Isador Grunthal of Jacksonville, and Raphael Moses and Henry Brash of Apalachicola fought for the Confederacy. Philip Dzialynski sought refuge with his extended family in Madison, and Robert Williams took his family to Savannah. Those who were loyal to the Union stayed in Union-held Jacksonville and Key West.[61]

In May 1865 Judah P. Benjamin, Treasurer and Secretary of State for the Confederacy, escaped the Union troops with the help of President Jefferson Davis and David Yulee. Benjamin took refuge in Florida on his way to Havana, from where he later sailed to Europe. Disguised as a farmer on horseback, he arrived at the Gamble Mansion in Manatee County, where he was hidden until he could escape to Cuba. When the Civil War ended, the personal baggage of President Jefferson Davis and his family arrived at Yulee's Cotton Wood plantation.[62] Soon after, David Levy Yulee was arrested and imprisoned for more than a year at Fort Pulaski.

Florida was devastated by the Civil War. During the Reconstruction Period, trains from the North arrived regularly, but trade resumed slowly. Some Jewish newcomers helped to restore the economy. They also helped to lay the foundations of religious communal life.

Most Jews during this period were peddlers or small town retailers. They gravitated to communities in the northern and central regions of the state, such as Pensacola, Jacksonville, Orlando, Bartow, Fort Meade, and Tampa. Lewis Kahn and Caroline and Jacob Kahn moved from Philadelphia to Pensacola in 1865.[63] Leopold Furchgott and Samuel, Jacob and Morris Cohen arrived in Jacksonville in 1867.[64] By

1870 Jacob R. Cohen had opened stores in Bartow and Fort Ogden for the Peace River traffic and the cattle trade. In 1871 he persuaded Philip Dzialynski, his brother-in-law, to help him run the Bartow store. Then Cohen moved on and opened another store in Orlando in 1874.[65] Later Philip and Mary Cohen Dzialynski owned general stores in Fort Meade (1876) and in Tampa (1879). In Fort Meade the Dzialynskis established a hotel, invested in citrus groves and exported alligator skins.[66] In 1876 Lewis and Henrietta Bear came from Greenville, Alabama, to Pensacola and had five children. Lewis started a grocery store and supplied merchant ships.[67] The Maas and Rheinhauer families had been neighbors in Germany before they moved to Ocala in the mid-1880s. Both families opened stores which still carry their names today.[68]

Perceiving the metamorphosis taking place with the destruction of the plantation economy, these Jewish merchants capitalized on their kin and their old-country ties *(landsmenschaften verien)* to purchase goods and services from wholesale merchants in other states.

Economic opportunity during Reconstruction did have its limits. Hiring African-Americans to work in a general store was still taboo for many Floridians. In 1869, when Samuel Fleischman defended former slaves as freedmen, the Ku Klux Klan demanded he leave Marianna. Fleischman fled to Tallahassee to seek protection. His body was found on the road to Marianna.[69]

Prior to the Civil War, Jews seemed less willing to leave the protective shelter of an established Jewish community to seek fortune and success on the isolated frontier. Neither synagogues nor other Jewish institutions were present to strengthen Jewish identity. After the Civil War, German Jews established religious and social organizations, and as more eastern European Jews arrived, more communal institutions were introduced.

In 1867 Jews gathered for worship in Jacksonville at the home of Charles Slager, but no formal organization was established.[70] About the same time Beth El Congregation in Pensacola began meeting, and it received a charter from the state as the first Jewish congregation in 1878.[71] The Jacksonville group reorganized under the leadership of Morris Dzialynski, now the city's mayor, and formed Ahavath Chesed Congregation in 1882.[72] British composer, Frederick Delius, was the congregation's organist by 1885.[73] By the end of the century, six congregations had been established in the state: Key West, 1887; Ocala, 1888; Tampa, 1894; and a second

Jacob Raphael Cohen
(Top Left) Came from Savannah, opened stores throughout Florida in the 1860s-70s, and settled in Orlando. Helped write the Orlando City charter in 1875 and elected first alderman. Married Rachel Williams in 1877, moved to Tallahassee, and was active in politics.

congregation in Pensacola, 1899.[74] Cemeteries were founded in Key West in 1865, Pensacola in 1869, Ocala in 1873, and Tampa in 1894.[75] B'nai B'rith chapters were chartered in Pensacola in 1874 and in Jacksonville in 1877.[76] A Hebrew Benevolent Society was organized in Jacksonville in 1874.[77] Newspapers in Tallahassee and Pensacola in 1878 reported on elaborate Purim balls.[78]

The establishment of these Jewish communal institutions may have slowed the Americanization process, but only some and only intermittently. Some of the first German generation intermarried; others consciously searched for and found Jewish partners. For example, Philip Dzialynski was widowed in 1864 and had a Jewish burial for his wife. He then married Mary Cohen of Savannah. When they visited their family in Jacksonville from Fort Meade, they prayed at Ahavath Chesed. His brother, Morris, married Rosa Slager, the daughter of prominent Jacksonville Jewish merchant Charles Slager. Their sister, Helena, married Robert Williams, of Tallahassee, a cotton plantation owner.[79]

Hundreds of guests attended the 1886 wedding of Rosa Benjamin and Jacob Katz in Micanopy. The occasion was reported in a large front page story in the *Micanopy Gazette*. The rabbi was brought in from Savannah and arrangements were made for the Florida Southern Railway to stop in Micanopy to pick up the bride and groom for their honeymoon.[80]

Jews assumed civic leadership in many communities. Some served as mayors. In 1879 Henry Brash began three terms as mayor of Marianna. Morris Dzialynski served in Jacksonville from 1881 to 1883, and Herman Glogowski in Tampa from 1888 to 1892. DeLand's mayor in the 1890s was Michael Davis. Michael Fischel served in Ocala from 1900 to 1902, following the term of Charles Rheinhauer.[81] Jews were aware that Levy County (1845) and Yulee City (1852) were named after David Levy Yulee.[82]

Jacob Raphael Cohen helped to write the Orlando city charter and was elected alderman in 1875. Two years later, he married Rachel, a daughter of Robert and Helena Williams, and moved to Tallahassee where he became active in politics. In 1901 Cohen served as a delegate to the Democratic National Convention.[83]

Philip Walter, a resident of Jacksonville, served as tax collector, chief supervisor of elections and clerk of the United States Court of Florida. In 1885 he represented Duval County in the Florida Constitutional Convention.[84]

Like other Floridians, Jews joined fraternal organizations in their communities to network and to bolster their political ambitions. Some joined the B'nai B'rith; others joined the Masons. Aaron Zacharias, Isador Grunthal, Jacob Huff and Philip Hale were members of Jacksonville's B'nai B'rith; Max J. Heinberg, Laz Jacoby and I.B. Hirschman were members of Pensacola's B'nai B'rith.[85]

High Holiday services were frequently held in Masonic Temples throughout the state. In 1873 the Benjamins, the Foxes and the Rheinhauers of Ocala were Masons. Marcus Endel of Gainesville was elected Grand Master of Florida's Grand Lodge of Masons in 1893.[86] Isidor Cohen, an early resident of Miami, viewed such fraternal non-Jewish organizations as "bind[ing] heterogeneous groups into common brotherhoods," promoting tolerance and helping to "banish bigotry [and] racial antagonism."[87]

Florida's Jews were not marginal outsiders in the latter half of the nineteenth century. The tension between ethnic identity and Americanization resolved itself in the first two congregations of the state by the turn of the century. These congregations adopted classical Reform practices. They supported the 1885 Pittsburgh Platform, which included anti-orthodox statements and viewed America as a homeland.[88] Many Jewish Floridians were "American-Israelites."

Much of the growth in Florida after 1880 can be related to a land boom. In 1881 Hamilton Disston, a non-Jew, bought four million acres of wetlands, mostly between Kissimmee and Lake Okeechobee, from the government for twenty-five cents an acre on the condition that he drain the land. By 1885 a legislative committee could count no more than fifty thousand acres drained but awarded him more than one and one half million acres for his efforts. Had Disston been more fortunate, Jewish refugees from Russian pogroms may have benefitted. The Okeechobee Land and Improvement Company attempted to settle the refugees north of the Everglades.[89]

In addition to agricultural and real estate developments, transportation magnates began to look to Florida as virgin territory. Trains could not only transport Florida goods to Northern markets but also could lure passengers South for tourism. In 1881 Henry Plant completed the "Way Cross Short Line" into Jacksonville for through trains to Savannah, and shortly thereafter, the line reached Kissimmee. In 1884 he extended his line into Tampa and was instrumental in the industrial awakening of Florida's west coast. Henry M. Flagler, John D. Rockefeller's partner in Standard Oil Company, opened a link to St. Augustine from Jacksonville in 1885 on his railroad system, later called the Florida East Coast Railway. By 1888 Flagler provided continuous service from

Jacksonville to Daytona Beach, and by 1896 his trains steamed into Miami. In the 1880s and the 1890s, Flagler complemented his rail lines with spurs that stopped at his new hotels: Ponce de Leon in 1888 in St. Augustine, Royal Poinciana in 1894 in Palm Beach and Royal Palm in 1897 in Miami. Flagler single-handedly reshaped Florida's destiny as the state prepared to greet the twentieth century.

Other industries also prospered. In Ocala, the 1880s brought mining of phosphate beds. In 1883 Morris and Saul Benjamin, Israel Brown and William Fox established an ice factory using water from Howard Springs.[90] Charles Peyser began manufacturing El Tropico cigars in 1886.[91]

In the 1880s several Jews came by boat to live and trade in Punta Gorda on the southwest Florida coast. Goldstein and Wotitzky are names that remain prominent one hundred years later.[92] Between 1880 and 1900 Florida's population doubled from one-quarter to one-half million and the Jewish population rose from less than one thousand to three thousand.[93]

During the late nineteenth century small Jewish communities surfaced around the state. A sizable group of Jews arrived from a single European area. Many Jews from Iasi and Husi, Roumania settled in Key West. That immigration was precipitated by an accident. Joseph Wolfson was on a ship that foundered off the coast of Key West in 1884. He came ashore, found a small Jewish community, and sent for the rest of his family in Roumania to join him. The Lebos, Wolkowsky, Rosenthal, Fine, Engler, Rippa, Argintar and Aronovitz families followed him to Key West.[94]

Other Jews from Husi settled in the northern part of the state. In the 1880s Zella Kanner settled in Quincy with her husband, Frank Seligman. In the next dozen years, seven Kanner brothers and sisters came to Florida to live in the small northern and central towns of Sanford, Palatka, Orlando, Mulberry and Ybor City. Their orthodox parents, Samuel and Esther, joined their children in Sanford soon after the turn of the century. Most of the Kanners married cousins and most had retail stores.[95]

Similar chain migration pulled Jews from Pusalotes, Lithuania, to Jacksonville. Fearing pogroms and conscription into the army, and lured by tales from lonely cousins of the *goldene medina*, the Finkelstein, Schemer and Slott families emigrated to Jacksonville. Soon they established a Pusalotes *landsmanschaft* and organized their lives around its activities.[96] Not comfortable with Rabbi Wittenberg at Ahavath Chesed and the Reform ritual, they helped form B'nai Israel, an Orthodox congregation, in 1901.[97] The

Finkelsteins opened a kosher boarding house to meet the demand of newly-arrived and traditional immigrants.[98]

Other families from eastern Europe and Russia settled in small towns in north Florida, like Live Oak, and kept Jewish traditions. The Rubenstein, Weiss and Gibbs families hired a *shochet* to move from New York to Live Oak to kosher their meat and to provide their children with a Jewish education.[99]

The Jews became more visible with the building of Jewish institutions. Because they were concentrated in the mercantile sector and frequently dependent on their northeastern kin for the acquisition and distribution of goods, some of Florida's Jews became targets of anti-Semitism.

This was the very time when social anti-Semitism emerged openly in New York in the famous episode concerning Joseph Seligman. Seligman, an investment banker, was denied accommodations at the Grand Hotel in Saratoga Springs. The following year, 1878, the New York Bar Association blackballed a Jewish applicant. During the next two decades, the Protestant establishment, increasingly wary of the mass immigration of Roman Catholic Italians, Irish and Poles, was outright perturbed by the growing number of Jews. In 1881 less than 3 percent of immigrants entering the United States were Jewish. By 1900 Jewish immigrants hovered around 13 percent.[100] In twenty years (1880-1900) the Jewish population quadrupled from 250,000 to one million.[101]

Henry Flagler, a northern Protestant aristocrat, shared the sentiments of his milieu. Adopting Florida as his new home, he attached restricted covenants to his land sales.[6] In 1915, the year Leo Frank was lynched in Atlanta, Carl Fisher of Prest-O-Lite and Indianapolis Speedway fame offered places in the sun on Miami Beach only to a wealthy non-Jewish clientele.[7]

This imported hostility to Jews by Northern entrepreneurs and tourists and indigenous Ku Klux Klan members made Florida an unlikely haven for most Jewish immigrants. The 1891 Key West city council imposed a $1,000 peddler tax which motivated Jews either to move into store fronts or to migrate north.[104] The Progress Club, a Jewish social club, was organized in 1876 in Pensacola as a result of discriminating practices by non-Jews.[105]

Hispanic-Jewish encounters were not overcast by these developments. Both groups were perceived as marginal minorities and outside the Protestant mainstream of Presbyterians, Episcopalians, Methodists and Baptists. In the 1890s, when José Marti began to galvanize people for his Cuban independence

Beth-El Confirmation Class, Pensacola, 1902
Rabbi Isaac Wagenheim poses with class. Sitting (left),
Fanny Berlin Jonas; (right) Sarah Heinberg Michaelson.
Standing (left to right), Rene Dannheisser, Sol Levy,
Fay Heinberg, Gertrude Friedman, Bennie Heinberg
and Esther Guggenheim.

revolution, Jews who were in the tobacco industry in Key West and Ybor City (Tampa) joined other left-leaning activists who supported his cause. The prophetic tradition and liberation politics from the book of Exodus appealed to Jews and Cubans alike.

In Key West, Louis Fine lived next door to Theodore Perez, one of the supporters of José Marti. When Marti came to town to seek financial support, Fine helped rally the Jews and solicited his contacts in New York to donate money.[106] Some individuals responded with more than money. Sol Schwartz volunteered to fight. A few Jews settled in Cuba after the Cuban War of Independence.[107]

The growth of the cigar industry in Key West and Ybor City blossomed in the late decades of the nineteenth century. New York cigar manufacturers took seriously the article "Rush to Key West" published in *Tobacco Leaf* in 1885.[108] Key West had transformed the smoking habits of Americans by offering them "American" Cuban cigars. In 1888 some 129 cigar factories competed in Key West. They produced 100 million cigars in 1890. A good number of the workers and employers were Jews.[109]

The Spanish American War, like the Civil War, attracted Jews to the military, among them Max Heinberg and Max Bear from Pensacola and Mannie

16

Brash from Apalachicola.[110] The port at Key West hosted the battleship *Maine* and military camps arose in Jacksonville, Miami and Tampa. Rabbi Isaac Wagenheim of Pensacola's Temple Beth El may have delivered the first sermon in the nation to announce the war victory. Later he received a letter from the President of the United States acknowledging his efforts.[111]

Jews and Hispanics frequently discussed together the future of Cuba while working on the plantations and in the cigar factories. Alfred Wahnish of Tallahassee and Aaron Zacharias of Jacksonville were tobacco growers, while the Rippas of Ybor City and the Ottingers and Wedeles of Quincy manufactured and packed cigars.[112] The cigar industry provided a bridge between the two ethnic groups.

Jews were also active in non-Hispanic industries. These included Morris Wittenstein in the dairy business in Orlando; Simon Rosin of Arcadia and Saul Snyder of St. Augustine in the cattle industry; the Krissmans of Dade City in the poultry business; and Henry Brash of Apalachicola in sponge fishing.[113]

Between 1900 and World War I, Florida's economic life changed dramatically. During Governor Napoleon Broward's administration, a system of canals converted uninhabitable land into prime real estate.[114] The hotel industry flourished as the wealthy took increasing advantage of the American subtropics. Aviation history was made in Florida. The first night flight was made over Tampa in 1911, and the world's first scheduled commercial airline flew from St. Petersburg to Tampa in 1914.

The mobility patterns of Jews in Florida also changed in those pre-World War I years. Jews living in small rural northern communities moved into Jacksonville to strengthen their Jewish traditions. Marcus and Hannah Weinkle from Moffit and Israel and Rose Stein from Lake City are two families who uprooted themselves. In Jacksonville the Weinkles and Steins helped found many Jewish and Zionist organizations.[115] With Flagler's railroad branching south into Palm Beach and Miami, South Florida became increasingly attractive. With the exception of Fort Lauderdale, which was still a trapping ground for Seminole Indians, a Jewish presence became discernable in southeast Florida.

Isidor Cohen and Jacob Schneidman, merchants from the northeast, had followed Flagler's railroad south, stopping first in West Palm Beach.[116] Although there had been twelve Jewish merchants in Miami in 1896, only these two remained in 1900. Nearly all the residents had left during a yellow fever epidemic the previous year. When Schneidman died, his widow,

Ida, married Cohen. Their son, Eddie, was born in 1907. His ritual circumcision was Miami's first, and it made front page news. Rabbi Julian Shapo came from Key West to perform the *Brit Milah*.[117] Over the next decade the Cohens were joined by many Key West families, including the Schwartzes, Englers, Fines, Rippas, Weintraubs, Wolfsons and Wolkowskys.[118]

Some families migrated from Russia directly to Miami. Henry and Louis Seitlin, ardent Zionists, escaped from Russia in 1910 and were sent by the Hebrew Immigration Aid Society to Florida that summer to join a Zionist farm settlement in Homestead. The settlement soon folded, so Henry peddled stockings and sundries. In 1912 he opened the Boston Shoe Store in Miami. Soon he had saved enough money to send for the rest of his family. When Henry's sister, Rose, married Max Lehrman of Homestead in 1913, the Miami community celebrated its first Jewish wedding at the home of Morris Zion. Two years later, the Lehrmans settled in Fort Lauderdale.[119]

Louis Seitlin's wife died in 1912. Her remains were taken all the way to Jacksonville for burial. Her death inspired Miami's Jews to found their own congregation and cemetery. B'nai Zion, the forerunner of Beth David Congregation, was founded that year, and land was purchased for a Jewish cemetery. Religious services were first held in a vacant hall over Henry Seitlin's store and later in the city's Masonic Hall.[120]

Seymour Liebman has estimated that fifty-five Jews lived in Miami in 1915 out of a total population of 15,437.[121] That year Jacob R. Cohen and Julius Hirschberg, two Florida Zionists, visited Miami as part of their state wide campaign to raise money for the *Yishuv*. This early appeal raised $10,000.[122]

World War I had a direct impact on the state's economy. Aviation is an example. Five of the nation's thirty-five flying schools were in Florida: in Pensacola, Miami and Arcadia. Key West boasted a submarine and naval training station; Jacksonville and Tampa shipyards contracted for more than a score of steamers and steel ships. Jacksonville also housed an army training base.

Patriotic Jewish Floridians joined up, among them Max Argintar of Tampa, William Wolfson and Abraham Cohn of Miami, David Sholtz and Philip Rubin of Daytona Beach, Isadore Greenberg of West Palm Beach, Mack Katz of Fort Lauderdale, Louis Paul of Jacksonville and Jake Kahn and Bertram Dannheisser of Pensacola. Nearly two hundred Jewish Floridians served in the Army and Navy.[123]

Nell Lehrman Gibbs
Born in Miami in 1914. She moved with her family
to Fort Lauderdale in 1916 where her father, Max,
had a department store. She married Louis Gibbs
of Live Oak; they live in Tallahassee.

When the United States entered the war in 1917, the nation's foreign policy was isolationist. Anti-Semitism increased sharply. Congregation Ohev Shalom in Orlando was organized when the Jewish community was left out of a war bond rally.[124] Blue laws prohibited conducting business or trade on Sunday.[125] The Ku Klux Klan parodied the Miami Chamber of Commerce slogan, ''It's Always June in Miami'' to ''It's Always Jew'n in Miami.''[126]

At the turn of the century, Jewish Floridians sought an American identity first. In Pensacola in 1916 Jews participated in Mardi Gras festivities and Max L. Bear was selected as Carnival King.[127] The influence of German Jews who settled in Florida in the nineteenth century played a significant role in channeling Florida Jewish life towards American norms of behavior. Communities with a large enough population, Jacksonville, Pensacola and Tampa, had more than one congregation and offered individuals a choice between traditional or Reform Judaism. The Jewish population in 1920 approached seven thousand of Florida's population of one million.[128] In 1928, 40 percent of the state's ten thousand Jews lived in Jacksonville.[129]

With the 1920s, Florida entered a boom period that lasted until 1928. America's middle class grew in size, and Northerners, looking for areas for new investments, turned to Florida. Jennie and Max Cypen brought their family from Chicago to St. Petersburg and established a hog farm.[130] A movie industry grew up in Jacksonville during the silent era, drawn by the climate and scenery, but eventually it moved on to California. Louis Mendelson was one of a handful who took advantage of the new medium.[131] The citrus industry expanded to the south, eating up mangroves and fertile land alike. Among the families involved in produce and citrus were Shader, Morrell, Meitin, and Heller in Orlando; Cohen in West Palm Beach; Wishnatzki in Plant City; and Bornstein in Clermont.[132]

In the 1920s the expanding transportation industry combined with smart advertising campaigns to convince the American public that Florida's sunshine, leisure and real estate could be theirs. America was on the verge of becoming the major global power. Gold currency replaced the silver standard of Britain. The ''Roaring Twenties'' brought a promise of ''a chicken in every pot,'' industrialization, and mass movement from rural areas into cities. The children of the millions of immigrants who had come into the country at the turn of the century had high hopes of becoming new Horatio Algers.

Many sought out Florida and bought and speculated on land. Dreams were rekindled time and time again, and by the summer of 1925, land fever was epidemic. Miami families who later played a significant role in the Jewish community, locally and nationally, arrived. Among them were Max Orovitz, Stanley Myers and Nathan Stone.[133] Some of those who took advantage of this boom were Jewish immigrants who had been sent from New York by the Jewish Agricultural Society. In 1926 eleven Florida families received Jewish Agricultural Society loans to support farming enterprises.[134] Few speculators became millionaires, and most were left paupers when the land fever broke. Florida's natural resources of sun and water were not yet synchronized to the rhythms of modern technology.

Events in 1926 forecast future storms. That year there was a disastrous hurricane, a fruit fly infestation and a real estate panic that sent the state into a depression—three years before the rest of the country. Many Floridians, including Jews, moved around the state with the ebb and flow of the economic situation. The Jewish Agricultural Society was called on for loans.[135] The Jewish population in Key West, Sanford, and Ocala declined; Pensacola, Jacksonville and Tallahassee stabilized; Orlando, Tampa and Miami grew. By the early 1930s Miami had replaced Jacksonville as the Florida city with the largest number of Jews: five thousand.[136]

The largest of these communities, Jacksonville, Tampa, Pensacola, Miami, and Key West established a core of communal agencies and other Jewish groups that included local affiliations with national organizations. These were YMHA's, Jewish sponsored Boy Scout troops, B'nai B'rith, the American Jewish Congress, the Workman's Circle, the National Council of Jewish Women, Hadassah, Young Judea, and the Zionist Organization of America. Forerunners of modern Jewish Federations were established. Jewish community newspapers were founded: *The Florida Jewish News*, 1924; *The Jewish Digest*, 1926; *The Jewish Advocate*, 1927; *The Southern Advocate*, 1927; *The Jewish Floridian*, 1928; and *The Jewish Weekly*, 1930. The Jewish Publication Society enjoyed memberships from Jews across Florida.[137]

Throughout the state, some communities during these interwar years had enough Jews to establish their first congregation and other Jewish institutions. These latest communities to come of age were Daytona Beach, Hollywood, Sebring, St. Augustine, St. Petersburg, West Palm Beach, Sarasota, Fort Lauderdale and Miami Beach.[138]

In 1937 Hillel was founded by B'nai B'rith at the University of Florida. Descendants of the Ossinsky family, who had come to Jacksonville in the 1880s, have taken leadership roles in B'nai B'rith throughout Florida.

Jews continued to be active in civic life. Between 1920 and 1940, eleven served as mayors in a variety of cities: Kelsey City, West Palm Beach, Arcadia, Neptune Beach, Crystal River, Dade City, Ft. Pierce, Miami Shores, Pensacola and Tallahassee. Abram O. Kanner, son of Pauline and Charles of Sanford, represented Martin County, first as a representative (1927-1936) and then as a senator (1936-1941) in the Florida Legislature, and later as a judge.[139]

Samuel Yulee Way, a non-Jewish descendant of David Levy Yulee, was mayor of Orlando between 1932 and 1934, in 1938 and in 1940.[140]

David Sholtz, a lawyer from Daytona Beach, was Florida's twenty-sixth governor (1933-1936) after first serving in the State Legislature as a representative in 1917 and 1918. To further his political career, Sholtz hid his Jewish identity from public scrutiny. To deflect a smear campaign in 1932, Sholtz sang in an Episcopalian choir while his rabbi, Max Shapiro, tried to involve him in the Daytona Beach synagogue.[141]

In some areas where Jews had difficulty running for office, novel approaches were initiated. The David Levy Yulee Voter's League was organized in Miami Beach in 1932 to lobby for candidates. Early pioneers like Miami's Isidor Cohen were vehemently opposed to Jews creating their own political lobby. Rabbi Stephen Wise and Dr. Cyrus Adler, leaders of the American Jewish Congress and American Jewish Committee respectively, agreed with Cohen that it was not good politics to declare oneself as a Jew: "We would regard such a move as thoroughly reprehensible, un-American and in conflict with the best interest of the Jewish people."[142]

On the eve of World War II, Jews comprised fewer than twenty-five thousand of the two million Florida residents and the five million American Jews.[143] While Jews living elsewhere in the United States participated in many aspects of traditional Jewish life, Florida Jewry had few such opportunities. Although Jews in some Florida cities had links to national Jewish organizations, Florida Jews as a whole were weakened by their small number. Families were spread across the state through marriage. Outside of holidays and life-cycle events they had little contact. More often than not, it was business as well as ethnicity that drew Jews to one another.

The United States' entry into the war in December 1941 dramatically changed Florida. Tourist facilities were converted to accommodate troops.

David Sholtz
(Right) Son of Russian immigrants who settled
in Daytona Beach. Elected to Florida legislature in 1917
and served as Governor 1933-36.
Shown with President-elect Franklin D. Roosevelt
in a motorcade in Miami, February, 1933.

Within months 75 percent of the hotel rooms on Miami Beach were being used by the Army and Navy. The disruption of the tourist business and its allied industries was more than offset by the conversion of the state into military training camps. Jacksonville had a new naval air station. Key West housed a reactivated naval base. Airfields were established in forty other locations. One-fourth of all Army Air Force officers and one-fifth of its enlisted men trained in Miami Beach.[144] Every major resort city in Florida had some branch of the armed services nearby, and families of servicemen traveled to Florida to visit. They revelled in the climate, surf and palm trees.

Floridians living on the coast knew about war firsthand. Scores of ships were torpedoed by German U-boats between Cape Canaveral and Key West. Even ships in the Gulf of Mexico were not safe; a British tanker was torpedoed off Apalachicola.

New roads connected long isolated rural areas. Industries made use of technology, and imported workers to meet labor shortages caused by conscription. The citrus industry developed the frozen-concentrate process. Foreign migrant farm workers were lured to Florida by lucrative incentives.

Jews in Florida, as everywhere, were deeply affected by the war. Their European relatives had been targeted for annihilation by the Nazis. The Jews who emigrated to Florida in the nineteenth and the twentieth centuries understood the full meaning of United States' isolationist policy. They watched the *St. Louis* slowly cruise off the coast of Miami Beach in 1939 seeking a safe port, only to be turned away and sent back to Europe. Herbert Karliner, one *St. Louis* passenger, returned to Florida in the 1950s. He came alone. His family had perished in the Holocaust.[145]

Jews, as all groups, were involved in the war effort. Several hundred fought in the European and Pacific theaters, including Major Charles Rosenblatt and Nell Israelson Friedman of Tampa, Samuel Wolfson of Jacksonville, Joseph Wittenstein of Orlando, and Sidney W. Langer, Eugene Weiss, and Mitchell Wolfson of Miami.[146] Others who lived near the seacoast volunteered to watch for German submarines and to assist cargo ships that were attacked. They blacked out windows and provided resources for Florida-based servicemen. Ironically, hotels that previously had "restricted clientele" signs accepted Jews when requisitioned for the war effort.

The post-war population exploded. Florida's population approached five million in 1960. The Jewish population growth was even more dramatic: from fewer than 25,000 in 1940 it grew to nearly

The Mosaic Floridiana Judaica Collection (hereafter MFJC) includes over four thousand photographs, thousands of artifacts and documents and several hundred oral histories housed at the University of Miami. Much of the content of the introductory essay has been gleaned from this collection. Other primary resources include, among others, the American Jewish Archives, the American Jewish Historical Society Archives, the Yulee Collection of the University of Florida and the archives of the State of Florida. This essay is the first overview of Florida Jewry published from the MFJC. The analysis should be viewed as preliminary. A book on Florida Jewry is planned after the exhibit travels the state of Florida.

1. The literature on ethnic groups in general and on Jews in particular is extensive. See Stephan Thernstrom, ed., *Harvard Encyclopedia of American Ethnic Groups* (Cambridge, Mass., Harvard University Press, 1980); Thomas Archdeacon, *Becoming Americans* (New York, The Free Press, 1984); Leonard Dinnerstein and David Reimers, *Ethnic Americans* (New York, Harper and Row, 1988) and Nathan Glazer and Daniel Moynihan, *Ethnicity: Theory and Experience* (Cambridge, Mass., Harvard University Press, 1975). Jewish references are noted throughout the endnotes. Much of the discussion today regarding ethnicity is couched in the context of multiculturalism and the reemergence of ethnic nationalism. See especially Anthony Richmond, *Immigration and Ethnic Conflict* (New York, St. Martin's Press, 1988).

2. Will Herberg, *Protestant, Catholic, Jew* (New York, Doubleday, 1955).

3. Herbert Gans, "Symbolic Ethnicity: The Future of Ethnic Groups and Cultures in America," *Ethnic and Racial Studies* 2/1 (January) 1979, 1-20.

4. See Steven Cohen, *American Modernity and Jewish Identity* (New York, Tavistock, 1983) and *American Assimilation or Jewish Revival* (Bloomington, Indiana University Press, 1988).

5. *Florida Jewish Demography* 3/1 (December) 1989, 1 and Adrienne Millon-Levin, *The Changing Size and Spatial Distribution of the Jewish Population of South Florida* (Miami, University of Miami, 1988), M.A. thesis.

6. Florida has received the greatest number of Jews from the Snowbelt. See Ira M. Sheskin, "The Migration of Jews to Sunbelt Cities," paper presented at the Sunbelt Conference, Miami, 1985, unpublished.

7. *Ibid.,* Table One. Cf. *American Jewish Year Book* 43, 1942, 656.

8. The American Jewish Historical Society published a special volume to mark the occasion. Originally published in *Publications of the American Jewish Historical Society* XLVI/3 (March) 1957, 133-464.

9. Salvador De Madariaga, *Christopher Columbus* (New York, Macmillan, 1940). For an overview of current debate see Eugene Lyon's forthcoming article on Christopher Columbus, *National Geographic*, 1992.

10. Jacob Rader Marcus has published extensively on colonial and early American Jewry. Recently, *United States Jewry 1776-1985: The Sephardic Period 1776-1840* (Detroit, Wayne University Press, 1990), Volume One. Stephen Birmingham, *The Grandees* (New York, Harper and Row, 1971).

11. See Martin A. Cohen, *The Jewish Experience in Latin America* (Waltham, Mass., American Jewish Historical Society, 1972), 2 volumes, and Judith Elkin, *Jews of the Latin American Republics* (Chapel Hill, University of North Carolina Press, 1980). For a brief survey of the Sephardim in the Caribbean, Latin America and North America, see Daniel Elazar, *The Other Jews* (New York, Basic Books, 1989), 140-183 and 223-225.

12. Martin Cohen, *The Jewish Experience*; Cecil Roth, *A History of the Marranos* (New York, Schocken, 1974); and Seymour Liebman, *New World Jewry: 1493-1825* (New York, Ktav, 1982).

13. Conversations with Dr. Eugene Lyon, Center for Historic Research, St. Augustine Foundation. The Borderlands Project of the University of Florida and the University of Seville is currently evaluating links between Spain and Florida during the Colonial Period. Jewish trajectories from this research are reviewed by Dr. Haim Beinhart, The Hebrew University of Jerusalem.

14. Bertram Wallace Korn, *The Early Jews of New Orleans* (Waltham, Mass., American Jewish Historical Society, 1969) 23-29 and 274-276. See also his "Jews in Eighteenth-Century West Florida," in Samuel Proctor, ed.,

Eighteenth Century Florida: Life on the Frontier (Gainesville, University of Florida Press, 1976), 50-59. Mendes lived in Curacao on and off between 1758-1779. See Isaac S. Emmanuel and Suzanne A. Emmanuel, *History of the Jews of the Netherlands Antilles* (Cincinnati, American Jewish Archives, 1970), 2:661, 665, 699, 701-7, 829, 832, 1033 and 1069. Samuel Judah, Korn notes, is mentioned only once in the West Florida Papers and cannot be identified with any of the Jewish Judah families then in North America (*The Early Jews*, 274).

15. Korn, *The Early Jews*, 32 and 278, fn. 75. The Monsanto Chemical Company of St. Louis was named in honor of a descendent of this Monsanto family.

16. Korn, *The Early Jews*, 24-28.

17. *Ibid.,* 20.

18. *Ibid.,* 25

19. *Ibid.,* 26. In part, the migration of Jews into Florida was possible because of a freedom of conscience provision written into a 1766 Act which neither compromised their faith nor their Jewish ethnic networks. The Act was passed on December 22, 1766, by the House of Assembly of West Florida.

20. De Palacios married the widow of Nathan Harris and helped to lay the cornerstone of the wall around a new Jewish cemetery in Charleston. Korn, *The Early Jews*, 276, fn. 64.

21. His Jewish heritage has been suggested by Sandra A. Thomas, "Survivors, Speculators and Settlers: The History of the Jewish Presence in Pensacola" (Pensacola, 1990), unpublished paper, MFJC.

22. Korn, "Jews in Eighteenth-Century West Florida," 54.

23. MFJC.

24. Samuel Proctor, "Pioneer Jewish Settlements in Florida, 1765-1900," in Samuel Proctor, ed., *Proceedings of the Conference on the Writings of Regional History in the South* (Miami Beach, 1956), 83, fn. 4. David Moses, a Jewish merchant on Charlotte Street in St. Augustine, sold hides.

25. Charlton Tebeau, *A History of Florida* (Coral Gables, University of Miami Press, revised 1980), 198. Cf. A. J. Messing, Jr., "Old Mordecai-the Founder of the City of Montgomery," *Publications of the American Jewish Historical Society* XIII, 1905, 75.

26. Several scholars have noted different totals for the acres Levy purchased. Proctor in "Pioneer Jewish Settlements" quotes Lord's total of 53,900 acres. M. Lord, Jr., *David Levy Yulee: Statesman and Railroad Builder* (Gainesville, University of Florida, 1940), 4, M.A. thesis. Arthur Thompson, *David Yulee: A Study of Nineteenth Century American Thought and Enterprise* (New York, Columbia University, 1954), 5, Ph.D. thesis, gives the total amount as 36,000 acres. Leon Huhner, "David L. Yulee, Florida's First Senator," in L. Dinnerstein and M. Palsson, eds., *Jews in the South* (Baton Rouge, Louisiana, State University Press, 1973), 54, notes 45,000 acres. Footnote 9 on page 54 in Huhner's article revises the total to 50,500 acres. In an earlier Huhner article, "Moses Elias Levy," *Florida Historical Quarterly* 19 1941, 326, fn. 29, his total purchase is stated as 53,000 acres. Joseph Gary Adler, "Moses Elias Levy and Attempts to Colonize Florida," in Samuel Proctor and Louis Schmier, eds., *Jews of the South* (Macon, Ga., Mercer Press, 1984), 25, puts it at 52,000 acres.

27. Haim Beinhart, "The Transmigration of Menachem and his family in the house of the Inquisition in Toledo, Bartolome Gallego" *Zion* 55/2 1990, 172 (in Hebrew). See also Huhner, "Moses Elias Levy," 319, who assumes he was expelled from the Iberian peninsula.

28. Huhner, "Moses Elias Levy," 319-320. Moses Levy described the change of name to the editor of the St. Augustine *Florida Herald and Southern Democrat* as follows: "The family name was that of Yulee, but surnames are little thought of by orientals.... A Levite [Jew] is called by Levy" (February 24, 1846).

29. Huhner, "Moses Elias Levy," 320 and fn. 5.

30. Thompson, *David Yulee*, 5 and fn. 9.

31. Huhner, "Moses Elias Levy," 321 and fn. 8.

32. *Ibid.,* 322, 325, 326, 328.

33. Proctor, "Pioneer Jewish Settlements," 84-85. Proctor assumes the names are Jewish as does Huhner, "Moses Elias Levy," 328, fn. 38. With the exception of Hendricks, the MFJC can lend support to his assumption.

34. MFJC.

35. MFJC.

36. "Harby's Discourse - the Jewish Synagogue," *North American Review* 23 1826, 72. Cf. Proctor, "Pioneer Jewish Settlements," 97.

37. Letter by M. E. Levy to Isaac Goldsmid, 25th Nov. 1825. See Jacob Toury, "M.E. Levy's Plan for a Jewish Colony in Florida - 1825," in Lloyd P. Gartner, ed., *Michael: On the History of the Jews in the Diaspora* (Tel Aviv, Tel Aviv University Press, 1975), 3:32. Isaac Goldsmid was a Jewish baronet and a leader in the Anglo-Jewish struggle for political emancipation.

38. For a discussion of New Pilgrimage, see Joseph Gary Adler, "Moses Elias Levy and Attempts to Colonize Florida," 17-29. See also Elfrida Cowan, "Moses Elias Levy's Agricultural Colony in Florida," *Proceedings of the American Jewish Historical Society* 25 1917, 132-134. Moses' agent in London, England, was Frederick S. Warburg. See *Allgemeine Zeitung des Judentums* 132, 1868, 346.

39. Huhner, "Moses Elias Levy," 330.

40. David Levy Yulee papers in P.K. Yonge Library, University of Florida for Gratz correspondence. Thomas E. Cochran, *History of Public-School Education in Florida* (Lancaster, State Department of Education Bulletin, 1921), no. 1, 1 for Moses Levy's educational achievements.

41. John Forester, *Letters Concerning the Present Condition of the Jews* (London, 1829), quoted in Huhner, "David L. Yulee," 56, fn. 28.

42. Th. Thrush, *Letters to the Jews with a copy of a Speech said to have been delivered by Mr. Levy of Florida* (New York, 1829), quoted in Huhner, "David L. Yulee," 56, fn. 27.

43. "Discourse before the Society for the Education of Orphan Children" (New York, 1830). For Isaac Leeser, see the *Occident*, 1856.

44. Huhner, "David L. Yulee," 55.

45. See the Yulee collection correspondence between Moses and David, University of Florida.

46. Jacob R. Marcus, ed., *Memoirs of American Jews 1775-1865* (New York, 1955), 146-202; from Raphael Jacob Moses' autobiography.

47. MFJC.

48. B. Bloodworth and A. Morris, *Places in the Sun* (Gainesville, University Press of Florida, 1978), 69.

49. Estimate of the Jewish population is based on MFJC. The population of Florida is the census data.

50. Eli Evans, in his recent biography of *Judah P. Benjamin: The Jewish Confederate* (New York, The Free Press, 1988), states incorrectly that Yulee "renounced Judaism [and] converted to Christianity" (48). Evans' wish is to legitimate Judah P. Benjamin as the first U.S. Jewish Senator. There is no documentation in the Yulee papers in the P.K. Yonge Library that Yulee formally converted. Yulee's correspondence with his father after his marriage continues to be linked to their common Jewish heritage. See Moses' letters February 4 and May 7, 1848; David's March 7, 1848, and August 21, 1849. Judah P. Benjamin also married outside Judaism. His wife, Natalie St. Martin, was a Catholic. Eli Evans' biography paints a picture of Natalie that leaves little to doubt: "Natalie had summoned a priest to administer the last rites, providing her husband with a contact with the Catholic Church at a final moment when he could not resist" (399).

51. Charles Francis Adams, ed., *Memoirs of John Quincy Adams* (Philadelphia, 1877), xi: 155, and xii: 164. For David Levy Yulee's history, see Lord, *David Levy Yulee*; Thompson, *David Yulee*; Huhner, "David L. Yulee" and "Moses Elias Levy"; and the Yulee papers in the P.K. Yonge Library.

52. MFJC.

53. MFJC. See also Ruth Hope Leon, The History of the Dzialynski Family (Jacksonville, 1954), Jacksonville Historical Society Archives, Jacksonville University Library and Cantor Brown, Jr., "Philip and Morris Dzialynski: Jewish Contributions to the Rebuilding of the South," paper presented at the Southern Jewish Historical Society, Jackson, 1990, unpublished.

54. MFJC.

55. MFJC.

56. N. Glickstein, *That Ye May Remember: Temple Ahavath Chesed 1882-1982* (Jacksonville, Byron Kennedy Publishers, 1982), 18. See MFJC for cemetery correspondence.

57. Glickstein, *That Ye May Remember*, 18. Cf. Pleasant Daniel Gold, *History of Duval County, Florida* (St. Augustine, 1928), 345.

58. Yulee's outspoken and radical views on state's rights and slavery earned for him the title "Florida's Fire Eater." See *New York Herald*, October 11, 1886 (obituary). Cf. Huhner's documentation in "David L. Yulee," 68-70.

59. In early January 1861 Yulee met with Southern senators in a plan to form a confederacy. On January 5, 1861, in a letter to Joseph Finnigan he wrote: "I shall give the enemy [the Union] a shot next week before retiring." On January 21, 1861, he announced his resignation and the secession of Florida from the Union.

60. Charles Norton, *A Handbook of Florida* (New York, 1892), 233.

61. MFJC.

62. President Jefferson Davis arrived on May 22, 1865. See *Florida Historical Quarterly* 67/4 1989, 532.

63. MFJC.

64. MFJC. Cf. Glickstein, *That Ye May Remember*, 18.

65. MFJC. See also Brown, "Philip and Morris Dzialynski," 11-12 and 14.

66. MFJC. See also Brown, "Philip and Morris Dzialynski," 15-16.

67. MFJC.

68. MFJC.

69. *House Reports*, No. 22, vol. 13, 42nd Congress, 2nd Session, 80, 82, 291. Cf. William Watson Davis, *The Civil War and Reconstruction in Florida* (New York, 1913), 576, 604.

70. *Occident*, August 1867.

71. MFJC.

72. MFJC. Cf. Glickstein, *That Ye May Remember*, 21-22.

73. MFJC. Cf. Glickstein, *That Ye May Remember*, 24.

74. MFJC.

75. MFJC.

76. B'nai B'rith Archives, B'nai B'rith, Washington, D.C.

77. MFJC. Cf. Proctor, "Pioneer Jewish Settlements," 105.

78. MFJC. See also the *Weekly Floridian* March 26, 1878, for Tallahassee.

79. MFJC. See also Brown, "Philip and Morris Dzialynski."

80. MFJC. See also the *Micanopy Gazette*, July 8, 1886.

81. MFJC. See also the forthcoming article by H. A. Green on "Ethnicity and Politics: Florida Jewish Legislators."

82. Levy County was named on March 10, 1845, in recognition of David Levy Yulee's contribution. Yulee City is in Nassau County. Bloodworth and Morris, *Places in the Sun*, 26 and 62.

83. MFJC.

84. MFJC. Cf. Proctor, "Pioneer Jewish Settlements," 106.

85. MFJC.

86. MFJC.

87. Isidor Cohen, *Historical Sketches and Sidelights of Miami, Florida* (Miami, 1925), 62.

88. Glickstein, *That Ye May Remember*, 25-26 for Ahavath Chesed in Jacksonville; MFJC for Pensacola's Beth El.

89. MFJC.

90. MFJC.

91. MFJC.

92. MFJC.

93. *The American Jewish Year Book* 1, 1899-1900, 284, estimates 2,500 Jews.

94. MFJC.

95. MFJC.

96. MFJC.

97. MFJC. See also Glickstein, *That Ye May Remember*, 26.

98. MFJC.

99. MFJC.

100. Abraham J. Karp, *Haven and Home* (New York, Schocken, 1985), Appendix 3, 376.

101. *Ibid.*, Appendix 1, 374.

102. MFJC. See also the archives of the Historical Museum of Southern Florida, Miami.

103. MFJC. See also the archives of the Historical Museum of Southern Florida, Miami. Fisher's deeds had the following proviso: ''Said property shall not be sold, leased or rented in any form or manner, by any title, either legal or equitable, to any person or persons other than of the Caucasian Race.'' There were exceptions. John D. Hertz, founder of Yellow Cab, and Albert D. Lasker, president of Chicago advertising agency Lord and Thomas, bought land from Fisher.

104. Charlton Tebeau, *Synagogue in the Central City: Temple Israel of Greater Miami 1922-1972* (Coral Gables, University of Miami Press, 1972), 30.

105. MFJC.

106. Neale Ronning, *José Marti and the Emigré Colony of Key West* (New York, Prager, 1990), Gerald Poyo, *With All, and for the Good of All: The Emergence of Popular Nationalism in the Cuban Communities of the United States, 1848-1898* (Durham, Duke University Press, 1989) and Malvina and Seymour Liebman, *Jewish Frontiersmen* (Miami Beach, Jewish Historical Society of South Florida, 1980), 13. Liebman has incorrectly identified the photograph as Louis Fine's home. The home is that of Theodoro Perez, 1123 Duval Street. See Jean and Wright Langley, *Key West: Images of the Past* (Key West, Belland and Swift, 1982), 46. Louis Fine lived next door at 1121 Duval Street. See the *1893 Key West Directory*. Cf. Ronning, *José Marti*, 100.

107. MFJC. See also Robert Levine, *Tropical Diaspora: The Jewish Colony of Cuba 1902-1990* (University of Miami, unpublished manuscript), 13-14.

108. L. Glenn Westfall, *Key West: Cigar City U.S.A.* (Key West, The Historic Key West Preservation Board, 1984), 29.

109. *Ibid.*, 43 for the statistics.

110. MFJC.

111. MFJC.

112. MFJC.

113. MFJC.

114. It is interesting to note that the Dzialynski kin were still active politically. Gertrude Dzialynski, Philip's daughter, served as Governor Broward's personal secretary. Brown, ''Philip and Morris Dzialynski,'' 40, fn. 120.

115. MFJC.

116. MFJC. Cf. Liebman, *Jewish Frontiersmen*, 22.

117. MFJC. Cf. Liebman, *Jewish Frontiersmen*, 25-26. See *The Miami Metropolis*, July 17, 1907, for the ritual circumcision notice.

118. MFJC. Cf. Liebman, *Jewish Frontiersmen*, 27-29.

119. MFJC.

120. MFJC.

121. Liebman, *Jewish Frontiersmen*, 27. Cf. Tebeau, *Temple Israel*, 37.

122. MFJC.

123. MFJC. For the total number of Jews in the military from Florida, see the *American Jewish Year Book* 22, 1920-1921, 444.

124. MFJC.

125. *The Miami Metropolis*, December 22, 1896.

126. MFJC and Polly Redford, *Billion-Dollar Sandbar* (New York, Dutton, 1970), 141.

127. MFJC.

128. *American Jewish Year Book* 22, 1920-1921, 371-2.

129. *American Jewish Year Book* 30, 1928-1929, 111, 125 and 182.

130. MFJC.

131. MFJC.

132. MFJC.

133. MFJC.

134. American Jewish Historical Society Archives, Waltham, Mass. See *Jewish Agricultural Society*, Annual Report, 1927, 4.

135. *Ibid.*

136. The *American Jewish Year Book* 42, 1940-1941, 233 and 235 notes Miami has 9,000 and Jacksonville, 4,820 Jews. In volume 40, 1938-1939 Miami was noted to have 2,000 and Jacksonville 3,700. The *American Jewish Year Book's* statistics are noticeably different from the MFJC after 1930. See also Millon-Levin, *The Changing Size*, and Ira M. Sheskin, *Population Study of the Greater Miami Jewish Community* (Miami, Greater Miami Jewish Federation, 1982).

137. For dates of each of these organizations in the various communities around the state, see MFJC.

138. For the chartering of each of these congregations, see MFJC.

139. See MFJC and H.A. Green, ''Ethnicity and Politics: Florida Jewish Legislators,'' forthcoming.

140. Huhner, ''Moses Elias Levy,'' 333, fn. 59, and 345.

141. MFJC.

142. Letter of Cyrus Adler to Isidor Cohen, May 5, 1932.

143. See Ira M. Sheskin, ''The Migration of Jews.''

144. Tebeau, *A History of Florida*, 417.

145. MFJC. See also the Holocaust Documentation and Education Center, Miami.

146. MFJC.

147. Sheskin, ''The Migration of Jews'' and *Florida Jewish Demography* 3/1 (December) 1989.

148. Harold Mehling, *The Most of Everything* (New York, Harcourt, Brace and Co., 1960), 76.

149. Paul George, *Visions, Accomplishments, Challenges: Mount Sinai Medical Center of Greater Miami 1949-1984* (Miami Beach, Mount Sinai Medical Center, 1985).

150. MFJC.

151. MFJC. See also *American Jewish Yearbook* 60, 1959, 45. In Miami, Temple Beth-El was bombed on March 16, 1958. In Jacksonville, the Jewish Center was bombed on April 28, 1958.

152. MFJC.

153. MFJC.

154. MFJC.

155. MFJC.

156. MFJC.

157. Minutes of the Board of Governors Meeting, Greater Miami Jewish Federation, October 6, 1949.

158. MFJC.

159. Estimates by Solomon Garazi, President and Isaac Benharroch, Executive Director, Federation of Latin American Sephardic Jewry (FESELA).

160. See MFJC and H.A. Green, ''Ethnicity and Politics.''

161. *Florida Jewish Demography* 4/1 (December) 1990.

162. *Florida Jewish Demography* 3/1 (December) 1989.

163. For each specific reference see MFJC.

IMMIGRATION ROUTES

Cuban Immigration
The Brameister family migrated to Cuba
from Poland in the 1920s when immigration
quotas blocked their passage to the United
States. A decade later, they settled in
Palmetto and opened a grocery store.
The granddaughter, Rachelle Nelson,
is a cantor at a temple in Miami.
Courtesy of Sarah Nelson, Miami Beach

Diaspora refers to the global dispersion of the Jews from their homeland since Biblical times. Those Jews who can trace their ancestry to the Iberian Peninsula where Ladino was spoken are called **Sephardim**. Those from central and eastern European countries where Yiddish flourished are called **Ashkenazim**. Descendants of both of these groups comprise Florida's Jewish community.

Jewish immigrants include refugees from religious and political persecution and those seeking economic opportunity.

The items that immigrants brought with them to their new country reflect a heritage they wish to retain and those things that make them more comfortable because they represent memories of the "old country." These objects become precious legacies to their descendants.

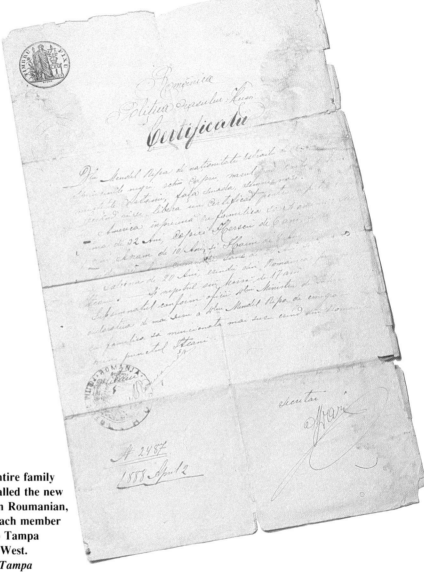

Roumanian Emigration Certificate
In 1888, Mendel Rippa immigrated with his entire family from Husi, Roumania, to Key West, which he called the new *medinat Yisroel*. This emigration paper, written in Roumanian, refers to Rippa of Jewish nationality and lists each member of his family. Some of the Rippas moved to Tampa when the cigar industry declined in Key West.
Loaned by Anne [Rippa-Solomon] Kantor, Tampa

Russian Samovar
Small brass samovar for making tea
in Russia. Samovars were often brought
by late 19th century eastern European
immigrants. This one belonged to
Ida Soclof of Pensacola.
Loaned by
Beverly and Marvin Kaiman, Pensacola

Lithuanian Passover Knife
Silver holloware table knife marked kosher
for Passover and "DT" for owners David
and Yetta Teitlebaum, Lithuania; now owned
by fifth generation family members.
Loaned by
Ida Koenigsberg, St. Petersburg Beach

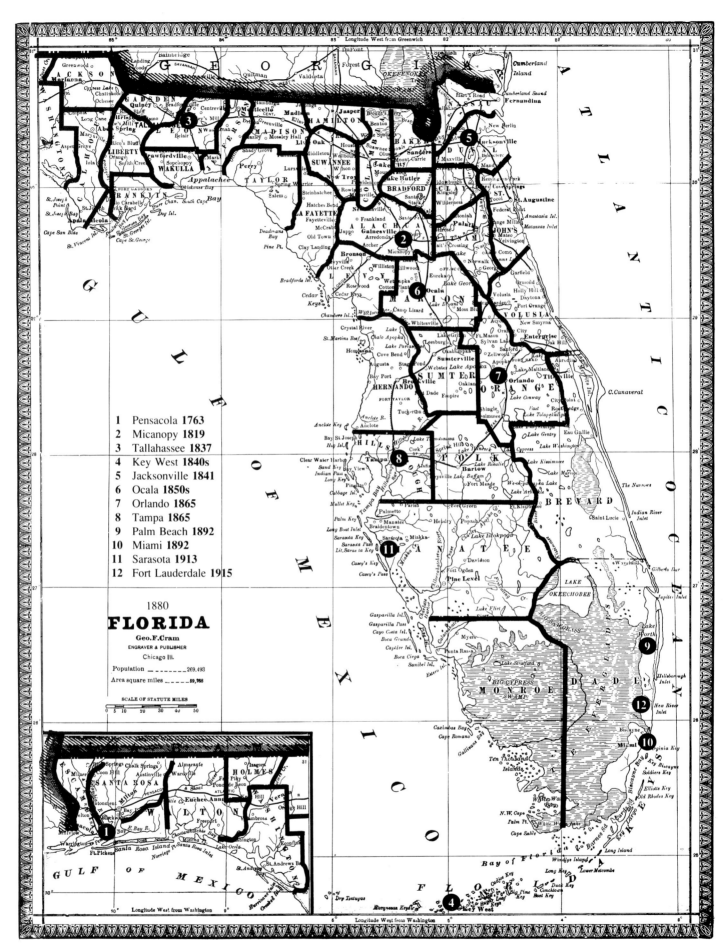

1 Pensacola **1763**
2 Micanopy **1819**
3 Tallahassee **1837**
4 Key West **1840s**
5 Jacksonville **1841**
6 Ocala **1850s**
7 Orlando **1865**
8 Tampa **1865**
9 Palm Beach **1892**
10 Miami **1892**
11 Sarasota **1913**
12 Fort Lauderdale **1915**

1880

FLORIDA

Geo.F.Cram

ENGRAVER & PUBLISHER

Chicago Ill.

Population _ _ _ _ _ _ _269,493

Area square miles _ _ _ _ _59,268

SCALE OF STATUTE MILES
0 5 10   20   30   40   50

Jewish Immigration into Florida from 1763
Courtesy of Historical Association of Southern Florida

30

LIFEWAYS

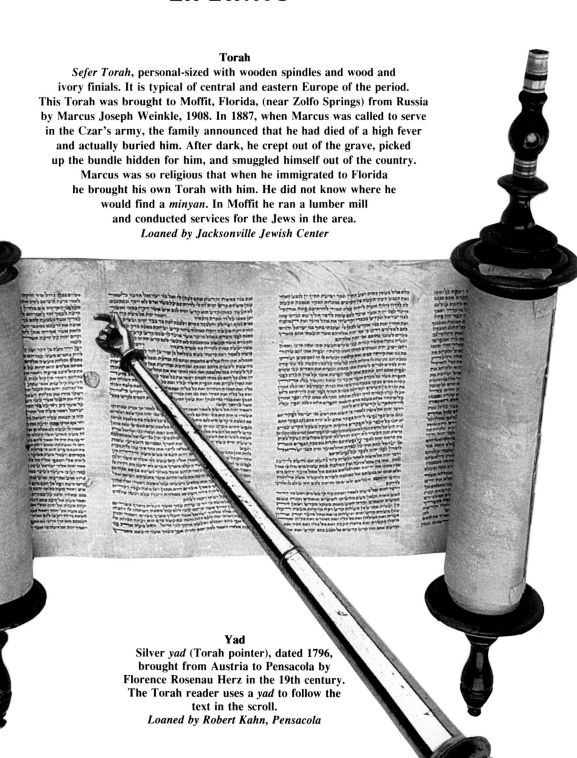

Torah
Sefer Torah, personal-sized with wooden spindles and wood and
ivory finials. It is typical of central and eastern Europe of the period.
This Torah was brought to Moffit, Florida, (near Zolfo Springs) from Russia
by Marcus Joseph Weinkle, 1908. In 1887, when Marcus was called to serve
in the Czar's army, the family announced that he had died of a high fever
and actually buried him. After dark, he crept out of the grave, picked
up the bundle hidden for him, and smuggled himself out of the country.
Marcus was so religious that when he immigrated to Florida
he brought his own Torah with him. He did not know where he
would find a *minyan*. In Moffit he ran a lumber mill
and conducted services for the Jews in the area.
Loaned by Jacksonville Jewish Center

Yad
Silver *yad* (Torah pointer), dated 1796,
brought from Austria to Pensacola by
Florence Rosenau Herz in the 19th century.
The Torah reader uses a *yad* to follow the
text in the scroll.
Loaned by Robert Kahn, Pensacola

The Torah is the most sacred text of Judaism.

The Torah encompasses the teachings of Judaism, its laws, doctrines, ethics, philosophy, ceremonies, and customs. The Torah designates holidays throughout the year as community and family celebrations to ritualize the life cycle and reinforces Jewish peoplehood. Rosh Hashanah, the beginning of the Jewish year, is followed by Yom Kippur, the Day of Atonement.

Then come Succot (Festival of Booths), Passover (Festival of Freedom), and Shavuot (Giving of the Torah) -- all historical agricultural festivals that are observed today through special rituals and prayers. Chanukah and Purim have been added as joyous festivals of survival. Shabbat (Sabbath), observed from twilight on Friday to sunset on Saturday, renews and reaffirms a Jew's identity, beliefs, and commitments through a weekly cycle. Jewish life is a continuous series of cycles and the individual life cycle is at its core, with birth, Bar/Bat Mitzvah, marriage, and death as the most significant rites of passage.

Shofar
Shofar, or ram's horn, blown as part of the New Year's ceremony on Rosh Hashanah and at the conclusion of Yom Kippur. This particular shofar has been used in Florida since the turn of the century.
Loaned by
Congregation Ohev Shalom, Orlando

Kiddush Cup
Kiddush cup, used for Sabbath prayers over wine. This one, coin silver, repousée, and chased, has engraving: "D[avid] Gundersheimer from A. Forcheimer, presented at the *brit milah*." These two families came to Pensacola in the 1850s and have descendents living in Florida today.
Loaned by Janice G.S. Brewton, Pensacola

Tenach
Confirmation Bible, ornate ivory and metal
cover, printed in Vienna, 1911, presented to
Ida Schwartz, Miami, June 15, 1924, by
Rabbi J. Shapo, Beth David Synagogue, and
Mrs. Isidor (Ida) Cohen, Principal.
Loaned by Clara Fine, Miami.

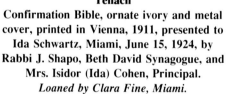

Mezuzah
Contemporary mezuzah, made in Israel.
A Jewish home differs in outward
appearance from those around it because of
the mezuzah that is affixed to the doorpost.
Inside the mezuzah Jewish prayers are
inscribed. The first, the *Shema*, begins,
"Hear O Israel the Lord our God is One, "
and another...."You shall inscribe them
on the doorposts (mezuzot) of your house and
on your gates" (Deut. 6:4-9). Some
Florida Jews buy their mezuzot in Israel.
Loaned by Dorothy Rombro, Casselberry

Community Wedding Rings
These rings, 19th century from central
Europe, were worn by the bride at her
wedding and the week following but were
owned by the synagogue. The band is
inscribed *mazel tov* and it has a house
perched on top that opens to hold a prayer.
*Loaned by
Sylvia and Jack Shorstein, Jacksonville.*

Kosher Plate
Porcelain plate, floral pattern with gilt border;
one of a Passover set which Henrietta and Henry Brash
koshered in the Gulf of Mexico at Apalachicola in 1865.
They built a home there and had eleven children;
descendants [Philipsons] continue to live in Florida.
Loaned by Erna Philipson Ferster, Fort Lauderdale

Yarmulke
Yarmulke (skullcap), hand-crocheted in
wool yarn by Rachel Kanner of Orlando
for her son, Aaron M. Kanner, 1907.
The yarmulke was entered
in the Orange County Fair.
Loaned by Marcia and Lewis Kanner, Miami

FAMILIES

Making a home and rearing a family are among the most important commandments for Jews.

Jews followed the same settlement patterns as other Floridians, going where economic opportunities and growth potential were greatest. Prior to World War II the Jewish population in Florida was sparse, under 25,000. Maintaining traditions in such settings required extraordinary commitment and resourcefulness.

The Mendelson Shrine Band
Reba Belle and Joel Mendelson try out their dads' hats and strike up a tune in 1921.
Courtesy of
Gertrude and Maynard Abrams, Hollywood

Dixie Flyer
One of the railroad "specials" that connected Florida to the rest of the United States. Annie Rosner and Ben Fleet of Live Oak were passengers in 1913.
Courtesy of Gertrude and Maynard Abrams, Hollywood

L'Shanah Tovah
(Left) New Year's card, 1904, from
Morris Daniels in Palatka. He married
Rose Kanner of Mulberry, one of eight
siblings who emigrated from Husi,
Roumania, to Florida.
*Courtesy of
Rose Kanner and Albert Friedman, Miami*

Dzialynski Pocket Watch
(Right) Pocket watch with hours in Hebrew and *bas-relief*
of Moses with the Ten Commandments on reverse,
owned by George Dzialynski (1857-1937), who was born
and died in Jacksonville. His father, Philip, came to
Jacksonville in 1850. His uncle, Morris Dzialynski, was mayor of
Jacksonville and founding president of Ahavath Chesed in 1882.
The family still lives in Jacksonville.
Loaned by Rosalie and Robert Coleman, Jacksonville

Gundersheimer Family
One of the oldest Jewish families in the state, Joseph Gundersheimer emigrated
from Bavaria in the 1850s and settled first in Milton, then in Pensacola.
During the Civil War, he accepted Confederate script in his dry goods store.
The eldest daughter, Carrie (center), was born in Milton in 1861.
There are descendants living in Pensacola and Sarasota.
Courtesy of Ann and Harold Schops, Pensacola

Kahn Family
Four generations of the Lewis and Sidonia Simon Kahn family in Pensacola are shown in 1890: Amalie Bloom Simon (left), her daughter Sidonia (right), her daughter Nettie Kahn Cahn (standing), who was born in 1867, and her daughter Renie Cahn (child). Widowed at a young age, Sidonia had a shoe store on Palafox Street.
Courtesy of Harry Kahn, Pensacola

Orlando Families
The Shader-Meitins and Wittensteins savor a swim at Wekiva Springs near Orlando in 1926. The families were neighbors in Pittsburgh and settled in Orlando in 1912. They were in dairy and citrus farming. The families continue to be very involved in community life today.
Courtesy of
Anne and Stanley Shader, Orlando

38

Ketubah
This wedding contract belongs to Margaret
Fishler and Joel Fleet, Jacksonville, and is dated
November 10, 1940. In Aramaic and English.
Loaned by Margaret and Joel Fleet, Jacksonville

BUILDING COMMUNITY

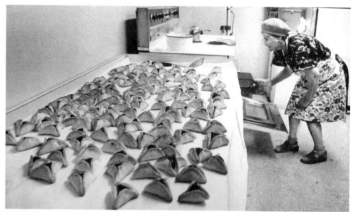

YMHA
(Top) In the late 19th and early 20th
centuries, prior to Jewish Community
Centers, Young Men's Hebrew Associations
(YMHAs) grew in response to the expanding
secular needs of Jewish communities.
This group in Key West enjoys an outing on
the Atlantic coastal waters in 1908.
Courtesy of Jack Einhorn, Key West

Mitzva Mobile
(Bottom) The Lubavitch is the best known
of the Hasidic sects of Judaism. They use
their *Mitzva* Mobile to convert other Jews
to their interpretation of Orthodoxy.
Courtesy of The Miami Herald

Purim Treats
(Top) Sylvia Elberg bakes *Hamentaschen*
(pastry for Purim) to help raise funds
for AMIT Zionist Women in Miami.
Courtesy of The Miami Herald

Temple Beth El
(Bottom) The first Temple to receive a charter in
Florida was (Reform) Beth El in Pensacola
in 1878. This building was constructed after
the first was destroyed by fire in 1895.
Courtesy of T. T. Wentworth Museum, Pensacola

"You shall not separate yourself from the congregation (community)." *(Mishnah, Avot 2:5)*

Within the community, the synagogue has served three functions. It has been a place of worship, where the community comes together to raise its collective voice to God; of education, where learning enhances the ability to understand the commandments of Jewish life; and of assembly, where all may meet to share in community activities. In areas and times when there were no synagogues available, services were held in homes or meeting halls.

In Florida Jewish communities, everything from welfare to vocational training, aged and child care, schools, cultural and recreational activities, health care, and refugee programs are provided by many organizations and synagogues. Funds are raised within the community to support these activities.

Super Sunday
Jewish Federation *phon-a-thons*
are conducted annually to
reach out for financial support
for local, Israel, and worldwide Jewish needs.
Courtesy of United Jewish Appeal

Sofer
The *sofer* (professional Torah scribe)
must possess a vast amount of Talmudic
knowledge and calligraphic expertise to be
entrusted with writing a Torah. Each Torah
needs to be written by hand and every word
must be perfect.
*Courtesy of Central Agency for Jewish
Education, Fort Lauderdale*

Synagogue Ark Ornament
Wooden pediment, carved, painted, and gilded from the ark of B'nai Israel
Synagogue, Pensacola, chartered 1899. The ornament depicts the tablets
of Moses flanked by the lions of Judah in an unusual running position.
This was in use in the 1920s through 1960s.
Loaned by B'nai Israel Synagogue, Pensacola

LAND OF OPPORTUNITY

People come to Florida for the climate, the ability to make a living, the lifestyle, or to be near relatives. For them all, Florida is a land of opportunity where their economic pursuits have no limitations.

Many bring special crafts and skills and infuse them into the Florida setting. Jews are involved in everything from shrimp and sponge fishing, tobacco and citrus farming, cattle and cotton, to wholesale and retail businesses and the professions.

Patriotic Button
Charles Ludwig immigrated from Iasy, Roumania, to Fernandina, in 1920, where he started a fishing fleet. Proud to be an American and optimistic about the opportunities ahead in Florida, he had this button made to display his patriotism.
Loaned by Anna Ludwig, Miami

Showtime
"Look Ma, I'm in the movies!"
Louis Mendelson sent this postcard to his Mother in Live Oak in 1910.
He was making a movie for
the Kalem Company in Jacksonville.
Courtesy of
Gertrude and Maynard Abrams, Hollywood

Plantation Bell
Alfred Wahnish left Morocco ca. 1890 and made his way to Tallahassee to grow tobacco. This bell was used for calling workers in for meals at the Wahnish plantation.
Loaned by
Ervin and Jacqueline Wahnish, Orlando

Produce Crate
Polish immigrants Harris and Yetta Wishnatzki came to
Plant City in 1930, after Harris had been a fish and produce
peddler in New York. A committed Jew, he designed his label
with a Magen David (Star of David), in spite of threats from
his competition. The family still uses the label today
on all the produce it distributes to supermarkets.
Courtesy of Wishnatzki and Nathel, Plant City

Hebrew/English Citrus Label
Can you read this? In the early days citrus
crates were shipped without identification.
Later, paper labels were glued to ends of the
crates to distinguish individual growers. This
early form of advertisement was replaced in
the 1960s by cardboard boxes. This shipper
was obviously attempting to appeal to the
Jewish market, as his label says *Florida* in
Hebrew.
Courtesy of
Museum of Florida History, Tallahassee

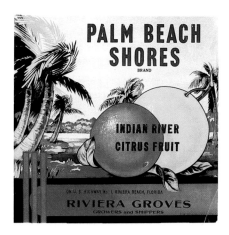

Citrus Label
The citrus industry is and has been one of
the primary bases of the state's economy,
although changing climatic conditions have
steadily forced it southward since the "Great
Freeze of 1894." The Cohen family sold
oranges under this label at their Riviera
Groves in Palm Beach in the 1930s.
Courtesy of Larry Cohen, Palm Beach

Young Entrepreneur
Aurel Rosin was following in his father's footsteps in 1915.
Simon had come to Arcadia in 1905 and developed a 4,500 acre cattle ranch.
Aurel grew up to be an attorney in Sarasota. He and his wife Elsie had
four sons: two physicians, (Alexander of Jacksonville and Michael of Sarasota);
and two lawyers (Robert and Simon of Sarasota).
Courtesy of Susan Rosin, Sarasota

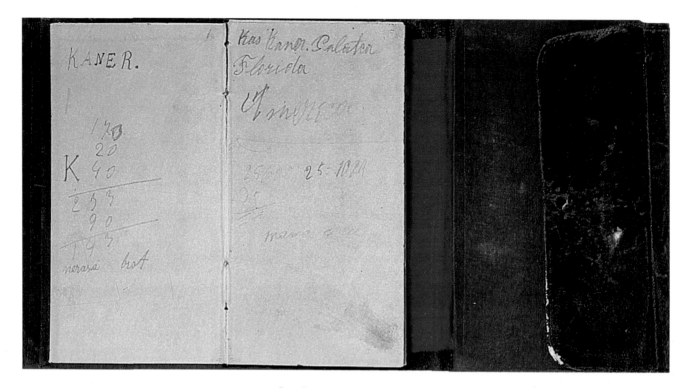

Immigrant's Notebook
When Harry Kanner emigrated from Husi, Roumania, in 1900,
the young immigrant practiced his name in English and the words
"Palatka," "Florida," and "America." His seven brothers and sisters
lived in small towns in central and north Florida. Harry settled
in Orlando, opened a store, and had sulky race horses.
Loaned by Marcia and Lewis Kanner, Miami

Cigar Factory
"We don't keep 'em - we sell 'em - PDQ" was
the slogan of Rippa Brothers Cigars, Tampa,
1909. David L. Rippa's family emigrated
from Roumania to Jacksonville, then moved to
Key West in the 1890s and to Tampa in 1906.
*Courtesy of Heléne Herskowitz and
Renée Bernard, Miami*

Frank's Clothing Store, Ocala
Julius and Julia Frank settled in Miami in the 1890s.
After Julius was killed in a fire in 1896, Julia moved with her
children, first to West Palm Beach and then to Ocala.
Marcus, a son, opened this store in 1905. He served in
city government for four decades and in the state
legislature in 1939 and 1949. He was so well respected that he
received 800 votes in an election after he died! There have been
five generations of the Frank family living in Florida.
Courtesy of Elka and Stanley Malaver, Ocala

Blanck's Department Store
P.G. Blanck married Jennie Rippa in Key West,
moved to Miami, and opened this
popular store in downtown Miami in 1913.
Courtesy of Doris and Bernie Blanck, Miami

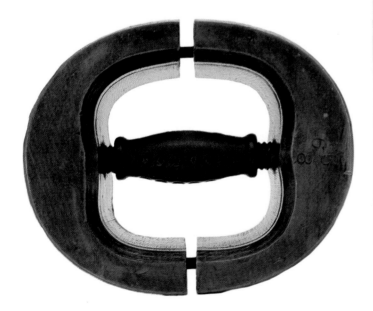

Hat Blocker
Wooden hat blocker (for shaping hats) ca. 1910, Guarantee
Clothing and Shoe Company, Ocala, owned by Joseph Malaver,
a Polish immigrant. The family continues to live in Ocala.
Loaned by Elka and Stanley Malaver, Ocala

Wolfson Political Campaign
Mitchell Wolfson campaigned and won a seat on the Miami Beach
City Council in 1939. In 1943 he was elected the first Jewish
mayor of Miami Beach, but he soon resigned to enlist
in the army to fight Hitler. Mitchell's father, Louis, had come to
Key West in the 19th century. By 1925 Mitchell and his
brother-in-law, Sidney Meyer, had created WOMETCO,
a chain of movie theaters, which in 1949, opened the first
television station in Florida, WTVJ, channel 4.
Courtesy of Louis Wolfson III, Miami

Farmers
Israel Shader (center) and his sons Myer (L) and Isadore (R) opened
Fairvilla Dairy in Orlando in 1913. Israel was a traditionalist in his
religious observances. Neighbors supported his beliefs by milking his cows
each week on the Sabbath when Jewish law prohibits work.
Courtesy of Ruth Esther and Joseph Wittenstein, Orlando

Peddler
Many immigrants peddled in Florida until they could afford to rent
or purchase stores. This rare photograph shows William Schemer, who came
from Pusalotes, Lithuania, selling fish on a Jacksonville street in 1906.
Courtesy of Vina and William Schemer, Jacksonville

FACES OF FREEDOM

Tradition commands that Jews work toward *tikun olam*, a just society. Jewish determination to repair the world and to secure personal freedoms has taken many forms: challenging prayer in public schools, fighting anti-Semitism and discrimination, and sponsoring programs that call for equal justice.

Jews, with other groups, respond to the call to defend their country and struggle to eradicate bias and promote understanding among all ethnic, political, and religious groups.

Cuban Passport
When Fidel Castro came to power in Cuba, about 3,000 Jews fled to Miami. Cuban passport of Elisa Gerskes, who immigrated from Poland to Cuba, 1917, and to Miami, 1962, to join daughter, Eva.
Loaned by Eva and Steven Feig, Miami

Spanish-American War Medal
(Above) One of Henry and Henrietta Brash's children, Mannie, served his country in the Spanish-American War.
Loaned by
Erna Philipson Ferster, Fort Lauderdale

Helping Refugees
(Top Left) Members of the National Council of Jewish Women assisted in absorbing Jewish refugees from communist Hungary in the 1950s, and continue today to help Latin and South American refugees.
Courtesy of
National Council of Jewish Women

Civil Rights
(Bottom Left) In 1964 rabbis were arrested with African Americans during a civil rights protest march against discrimination in Tallahassee.
Courtesy of Florida Photographic Collection,
Department of State, Tallahassee

Soviet Jewry Button
(Above) In the Soviet Union after
World War II, there were severe
restrictions on Jews emigrating and a
ban against practicing Judaism.
This denial provided a focus for Jewish
activism in Florida for decades.
Today Jewish communities are resettling
Soviet immigrants.
Loaned by Eva and David Ritt, Maitland

World War I Veteran
(Right) Herman D. Adelstein earned the
Silver Star, America's second-highest medal
for bravery in World War I. Superiors
blocked the award because he was a Jew.
Sixty years later, Florida's United States
Senator Richard Stone set the
record straight and pinned on
Herman's long-overdue medal.
*Courtesy of Jewish War Veterans Archives,
Washington, D.C.*

Civil War Certificate
(Bottom Right) A Daughters of the Confederacy
certificate is proudly owned by
Erna Philipson Ferster, whose grandfather,
Henry Brash, served in the Civil War.
The family settled in Apalachicola in 1865.
*Loaned by
Erna Philipson Ferster, Fort Lauderdale*

51

SEPHARDIM

Jews who trace their ancestry to the Iberian Peninsula before the expulsion from Spain in 1492 are called **Sephardim**. Many Sephardic Jews were among the earliest to settle the New World in such places as Mexico, Curacao, and Cuba. Some who chose conversion in order to remain in Spain may have come to Florida with early Spanish explorers. Florida's earliest Jews (1763) were Sephardic. Since World War II, the political climate in Latin America has motivated several thousand **Sephardim** to immigrate to Florida.

Bishola

Sephardic custom includes a *bishola* **(naming ceremony) for girls at least one month old. The "bride" is the child's godmother, a virgin, who presents her to the rabbi. Here, Luisa Behar holds Blanca Garazi, Havana, 1958, shortly before the Garazi family escaped to Florida.**
Courtesy of Esther and Solomon Garazi Lilo, Miami

52

Mirror Amulet
Many customs concern protection against
the "evil eye." Mirrors hung throughout
the house deflect malice. This ornate silver
version is in modern Sephardic style from Turkey.
Loaned by Esther and Solomon Garazi Lilo, Miami

Garlic Amulet
Sephardic folk custom called for small bags
of garlic to be hung on a crib or in an
infant's room to protect against the evil spirit.
Loaned by Esther and Solomon Garazi Lilo, Miami

53

Hamsa
The *hamsa* (hand) is an amulet that wards
off evil. Five is a powerful number.
This one, Sephardic style from North Africa,
is brass ornamented with glass beads and the
Magen David (Star of David).
Loaned by Esther and Solomon Garazi Lilo, Miami

HOLOCAUST

Since 1945 several thousand Holocaust survivors have come to Florida. Many of their children and grandchildren live close by. Survivors continue to bear witness so that future generations will always remember the Holocaust and learn from it. Throughout the state there are Holocaust Memorials and Museums that provide programs and sponsor documentation and oral histories.

Survivor
Herbert Karliner was a boy traveling with his family
on the German steamship "St. Louis" on June 4, 1939,
looking for a Florida port to accept its 900 passengers.
After seeing the palm trees and hotels from afar,
Herbert promised himself that if he survived, he would
return to Miami Beach. He did, in 1954.
Courtesy of Herbert Karliner, Miami Beach

Stained Glass Memorial
Vera Sattler, Melbourne
artist and wife of Holocaust
survivor Max Sattler,
designed, painted,
and constructed this original
work of art for MOSAIC.
The window tells of the
transition from the hell of
the Holocaust to recovery
and the survival of Judaism.
Superimposed on the entire
window is the Yizkor prayer,
"a memorial to the
generations who sacrificed
their lives to sanctify
Thy God's name...."
*Gift of Vera and Max Sattler,
Melbourne*

ZIONISM

"Next Year in Jerusalem" has been a prayer and a rallying cry for Jews of the Diaspora. As the modern Zionist movement grew (post 1896), Jewish Floridians joined with others in making aliyah during the days of the *Yishuv*.

The creation of the state of Israel in 1948 was the culmination of the hopes and plans of millions of Jews, including many in Florida. Some helped to ship supplies and arms, and some volunteered to fight for the young country; others conducted appeals. Today Jews throughout Florida continue to support Israel by visiting and working there, by sending their children to study, by raising funds, and by making aliyah.

Israel Bonds
In the wake of the 1973 war against Israel, an emergency Israel Bond campaign is initiated.
Courtesy of Judaic Studies Collection, University of Miami

JNF Blue Box
The need to clear and develop the land and plant trees is especially acute in Israel. Blue boxes can be seen throughout Florida Jewish homes and businesses as a way to support the Jewish National Fund, which improves the quality of life for Israelis.
Loaned by Sandra and Neil Malamud, Sarasota

Moshav
Come visit Me'ammi - an Israeli cooperative settlement named after Miami.
Courtesy of The Miami Herald

Post-Camp David
Two statesmen, Florida's Governor
Bob Graham and Israel's Prime Minister
Menachem Begin, meet shortly after
the Camp David talks to exchange
views on peace in the Middle East.
Courtesy of Florida Photographic Collection,
Department of State, Tallahassee

Birobidjan
World events impact Florida Jews. In 1932 a group in
Pensacola organized to support Josef Stalin's plan for a Jewish
homeland in Birobidjan, USSR, established in 1928.
This photograph was a greeting card to the Soviet Union.
Courtesy of Max Bear, Pensacola

We Are One
Several months prior to Israel declaring independence on May 14, 1948,
Golda Meyerson (Meir) appealed to American Jewry for $50 million so that Israel could defend herself
against the Arab states. Stanley Myers of Miami, President of the Council of Jewish Federations (CJF);
Henry Morgenthau, national United Jewish Appeal (UJA) chairman; and New York Governor
Herbert Lehman joined Golda for the first UJA phon-a-thon.
Courtesy of Judy Myers Gilbert, Miami

Hadassah
Hadassah, a Zionist women's
organization, conducted its annual
membership campaign,
Florida style, 1950s.
Courtesy of Hadassah

59

SUNSET

Beginning in the 1880s Florida has been viewed as a paradise for those in their golden years. At first the "snow birds" were only the affluent. Then more and more flocked south to escape harsh winters. After World War II and the introduction of air-conditioning, retirees began choosing Florida as their number one sun destination. Many were fixed-income elderly seeking a place of peace and warmth in their sunset years. Some have had to cope with increasing poverty. Most seniors are involved, concerned activists. They come for the sun, but refuse to merely bask in it. They see a new kind of opportunity in Florida — not just for economic gain, but also for personal and communal growth.

Mah Jongg
This Chinese game helps
fill the day and generates friendships.
Loaned by Bonnie Cohn Levy, Orlando

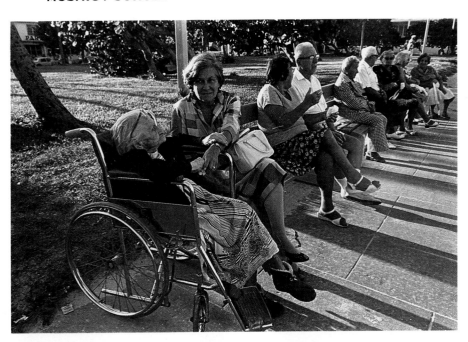

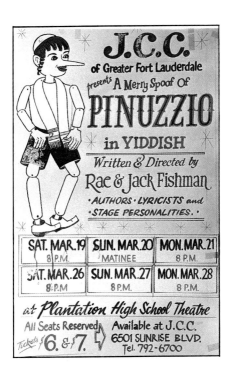

Jewish Pinocchio
Yiddish culture is alive and well in
Florida! At the Soref Jewish Community
Center in Fort Lauderdale, seniors are
reviving interest in the language and
culture with adaptations of classics.
Pinuzzio is Yiddish for Pinocchio.
Loaned by Soref JCC, Fort Lauderdale

Golden Years
There are about 330,000 Jewish seniors living in Florida. Retirement
migration is good for Florida and good for helping to fulfill a lifetime of dreams.
Courtesy of Gary Monroe, DeLand

FLORIDA JEWS
OR JEWISH FLORIDIANS?

Florida Jews or Jewish Floridians? That is an ongoing question. The process of Americanization is a struggle for balance. Each ethnic group comes with its own traditions and culture and each must face the challenges of integrating into a new society. The tension between preserving Jewish identity and acculturating into American society confronts every Jew. Each succeeding generation responds differently from their immigrant ancestors.

In this tropical setting, people of all backgrounds have found an openness to choose the intensity of their ethnic identity.

"A Bit of Florida"
In order to help tourists "send a bit of Florida back home,"
Rachel Luba Wilck, a Polish immigrant, bought baby turtles and
alligators from the Seminole Indians and shipped them
to all parts of the country in the 1920s and 1930s.
Courtesy of Joan Schwartzman, Miami

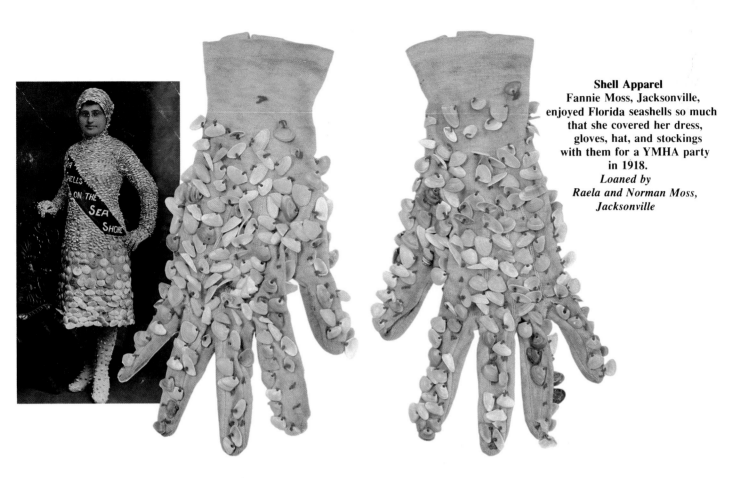

Shell Apparel
Fannie Moss, Jacksonville,
enjoyed Florida seashells so much
that she covered her dress,
gloves, hat, and stockings
with them for a YMHA party
in 1918.
Loaned by
Raela and Norman Moss,
Jacksonville

A Day at the Races
Al Jolson was one of the thousands who came
to Florida in the 1920s for "sun and fun."
Courtesy of Historical Association of Southern Florida

Mardi Gras
Max L. Bear was selected King of the Mardi Gras in 1916 for his contribution to
Pensacola's civic life. His father, Lewis Bear, had come to Pensacola
from Alabama in 1876 and founded a grocery business that continues to this day.
Max was Pensacola's mayor in 1937 and served as president of Temple Beth El for forty years.
Courtesy of T.T. Wentworth Museum, Pensacola

Afternoon at the Beach
In 1928 Mollie Robbins, Mollie Newman [Spier], Rose Reiss, Sadye Katz,
and her daughter Gloria [Rubell] enjoyed a day on Fort Lauderdale Beach.
These women were the pioneers of Temple Emanu-El, Fort Lauderdale.
Courtesy of the Katz Family, Fort Lauderdale

Tourism
Florida's waters enticed thousands in 1925.
Malvina Weiss offered a tempting invitation
on this Miami Beach brochure. Rose Weiss,
her mother, was a community activist and
was known as the "Mother of Miami Beach."
Loaned by Ruth and Eugene Weiss, Miami Beach

Gubernatorial Inauguration, 1885
Robert Williams came to Tallahassee ca. 1850 to grow cotton.
He married Helena Dzialynski of Jacksonville and they raised
five daughters. Mena, a daughter, is shown presenting a flag
(spun of Tallahassee silk) to Governor Edward Perry.
Courtesy of Isadore and Ethel Moscovitz, Jacksonville

"Kiss Me, I'm Jewish" Button
Loaned by Heather Cohen, Orlando

Jewish Introductions
Most of Jewish life focuses on the
family unit. Jewish communities are
responding to the needs of singles as
their numbers increase.
Courtesy of Evelyn Gross, Boca Raton

GLOSSARY

ALIYAH	Honor of being called up to the reading of the Torah; act of emigrating to Israel.
ASHKENAZIM	Jews originating from central and eastern Europe.
BAR MITZVAH	Religious majority for males at age of 13 (lit. "Son of the Commandment"; plural *B'nai Mitzvah*).
BAT MITZVAH	Religious majority for females at age of 12 (lit. "Daughter of the Commandment"; plural *B'not Mitzvah*).
BIMA	Podium; pulpit or reader's platform in the synagogue.
BISHOLA	Sephardic naming ceremony for girls.
BRIT MILAH	Ritual circumcision for male held on the 8th day following birth.
CHANUKAH	Festival of Lights commemorating the defeat of the Seleucids 2155 years ago and the rededication of the Temple.
CHANNUKIA	Chanukah nine branch candelabra.
CHESED SHEL EMETH	Name for Jewish Burial Society (*lit. "An act of true kindness"*).
CHEVRA KADISHA	Jewish Burial Society.
CHUPA	Wedding canopy.
CONVERSOS	Jews who converted to Christianity to save their lives under threat of death.
DIASPORA	Global dispersion of the Jews from their homeland, Israel, since biblical times.
ERUV	Boundary marking area where carrying objects on the Sabbath is permissible.
ETROG	Lemon-like fruit used during the holiday of Succot.
GENIZAH	Repository of worn or torn sacred Hebrew books or scrolls.
HAMENTASCHEN	Three cornered poppy seed pastries eaten on Purim.
HAMSA	Amulet, in the form of a hand, to ward off evil.
HASIDISM	Movement within Orthodox Jewry stressing religious fervor, joy and dedication to Jewish tradition and individual leaders.
HAVDALA	Ceremony marking the conclusion of the Sabbath.
KETUBAH	Wedding contract detailing mutual responsibilities of husband and wife.
KIDDUSH	Blessing over wine.
LADINO	Language originating in Spain combining elements of Hebrew, Spanish and Arabic.
MAGEN DAVID	Jewish symbol of six-pointed star.
MAGEN DAVID ADOM	Israeli organization similar to the Red Cross.
MARRANOS	Conversos and their descendants who practiced their Judaism secretly.
MATZAH	Unleavened bread eaten specifically but not only during the Passover holiday.
MAZEL TOV	Good luck.
MEDINAT YISRAEL	State of Israel.
MEZUZAH	Container holding Biblical portions, placed on the upper part of the doorpost.

MINYAN	Required quorum of ten adults for communal Jewish prayer.
MITZVAH	Commandment, good works (plural *Mitzvot*).
MIZRACH	Home sign or decoration denoting eastward direction indicating Land of Israel towards which prayers should be expressed.
MOHEL	Ritual circumciser.
MOSHAV	Cooperative settlement in Israel.
PASSOVER	Agricultural festival; commemorates the exodus from Egypt.
PAYOS	Sidelocks worn by some Orthodox males.
PIDYON HABEN	Ceremony of redemption of the first born son.
PURIM	Holiday commemorating the saving of the Jews in Persia.
ROSH HASHANAH	New Year.
SEDER	Festive Passover meal and home service.
SHANAH TOVAH	Happy New Year.
SEPHARDIM	Jews originating from the Iberian Peninsula (Spain and Portugal).
SHABBAT	Sabbath.
SHOCHET	Kosher ritual slaughterer.
SOFER	Professional Torah scribe.
SHOFAR	Ram's horn blown on Rosh Hashanah and Yom Kippur.
SHAVUOT	Agricultural festival; commemorating the giving of the Torah.
SHUL	Synagogue.
SUCCOT	Agricultural festival; Festival of Booths.
TALLIT	Fringed prayer shawl used in Jewish worship.
TALMUD	Rabbinic, legal and homiletical discussions on the Bible.
TEFILLIN	Set of two leather straps with box attached worn on the arm and head during weekday morning prayers, containing portions of the Torah.
TENACH	Five Books of Moses, Prophets and other Biblical Writings.
TIKUN OLAM	The repairing of the world to bring a just society.
TORAH/SEFER TORAH	Five Books of Moses; more generally broad spectrum of Jewish learning and study.
TZEDEKAH	Philanthropy or charity based on Jewish religious obligation to establish a righteous world.
TZIZIT	Fringes placed on prayer shawls and garments reflecting a Biblical command.
YAD	Pointer used in the reading of the Torah Scroll.
YAHRZEIT	Anniversary of the death when prayers are said for the deceased.
YARMULKE	Skull cap.
YIDDISH	Language originating in central and eastern Europe combining elements of Hebrew, German and Slavic tongues.
YISHUV	The Jewish community in the State of Israel.
YIZKOR	Memorial prayer said on major Jewish festivals.
YOM KIPPUR	Day of Atonement.
ZACHOR	"Remember" used especially in reference to the Holocaust.

MOSAIC INC.
BOARD OF DIRECTORS 1990-1991

LENDERS TO THE EXHIBIT

Gertrude & Maynard Abrams, Delray Beach
American Jewish Historical Society, Waltham, MA
Anne & David Anchin, Sarasota
Anti-Defamation League, Miami
Joseph Barbanel, Coconut Creek
Eunice Tall Baros, Miami
Blanche & Barney Barrett, Pensacola
Joanne & Dr. Robert Bass, Miami Beach
Rabbi Herbert Baumgard, Miami
Corene Bear, Orlando
Jack Becker, Jacksonville
Jackie Bell, Sun Sentinel, Lauderhill
Isaac Benharroch, Miami
Dr. Philip & Marilyn Benjamin, St. Petersburg
Renée & Marshall Bernard, Miami
Adele & George Bernstein, Miami
Doris & Bernie Blanck, Miami
Bonnie & Mark Blank, Miami
Rep. Elaine Bloom, Miami Beach
B'nai Israel Synagogue, Pensacola
Janice G. S. Brewton, Pensacola
Ann Broad Bussel, Miami
Marwin Cassel, Miami
Charlotte Weinkle Chazin, Sarasota
Claire & Barnett Chepenik, Orlando
George Chillag, Miami
Esther Neham Cogen, Miami
Heather Cohen, Orlando
Sylvia & Richard Cole, Pensacola
Gertrude & Colson Perry Coleman, Jacksonville
Rosalie & Robert Coleman, Jacksonville
Community Relations Committee,
Greater Miami Jewish Federation
Congregation Oher Shalom, Orlando
Douglas Gardens Home for the Aged, Miami
Helene & Murray Dubbin, Miami
Jack Einhorn, Key West
Gary Eisenberg, Miami
Eva & Steven Feig, Miami Beach
Erna Philipson Ferster, Fort Lauderdale
Clara Fine, Miami
Carolyn Wedeles & Arthur Fixel, Quincy
Margaret & Joel Fleet, Jacksonville

Florida Photographic Collection, Dept. of State, Tallahassee
Ida Engler Forer, Miami
Ann & Irving Frankel, Miami Beach
Albert & Rose Kanner Friedman, Miami
Nell & Herbert Friedman, Tampa
Fort Lauderdale News & Sun Sentinel, Fort Lauderdale
Esther & Solomon Garazi, Miami Beach
Rabbi Stanley Garfein, Tallahassee
Sheldon Gendzier, Jacksonville
Gladys Gerofsky, Ocala
David Gibbs, DeLand
Nell & Louis Gibbs, Tallahassee
Hedi Goldfarb, Orlando
Dr. Ruth & Arnold Greenfield, Miami
Ruth Frank Gross, Pompano Beach
Natalie Glickstein Haas, Jacksonville
Julia & Henry Halpern, Jacksonville
Lisette & Edward Halpern, Orlando
Irving Heller, Miami
Heritage Florida Jewish News, Orlando
Heléne & Bernie Herskowitz, Miami
Historical Museum of Southern Florida, Miami
Laura Kass Hochman, Fort Lauderdale
Jacksonville Jewish Center, Jacksonville
Dave & Mary Alper Jewish Community Center, Miami
Greater Orlando Jewish Community Center, Orlando
Samuel & Helene Soref Jewish Community Center,
Fort Lauderdale
Jewish Federation, Greater Miami
Jewish Federation, Jacksonville
Jewish War Veterans Archives, Washington, DC
Judaic Studies Program, University of Miami,
Coral Gables
Harry Kahn, Pensacola
Robert Kahn, Pensacola
Beverly & Marvin Kaiman, Pensacola
Marcia & Lewis Kanner, Miami
Cora & Jack Kanner, Sanford
Estelle & Harry Kaplan, Melbourne
Herbert Karliner, Miami
Rita & Jerry Kass, St. Augustine
Bunny & Abe Katz, St. Petersburg
Key West Historical Society

MOSAIC / LENDERS TO THE EXHIBIT

Ida Koenigsberg, St. Petersburg Beach
Sidney W. Langer, Miami
Florence Argintar Lebos, Tampa
Dorothy & Rabbi Sidney Lefkowitz, Jacksonville
Lehrman Day School, Miami Beach
Myrna Gordon Leonard, Miami
Dr. Robert Levine, Miami
Anna Kronberg Ludwig, Miami
Natalie Engler Lyons, Miami
Elka & Stanley Malaver, Ocala
Bluma Wise & Ralph Meitin, Orlando
Roberta Cohen Mendel, West Palm Beach
The Miami Herald, Miami
Gary Monroe, DeLand
Isadore & Ethel Moscovitz, Jacksonville
Raela & Norman Moss, Jacksonville
Museum of Florida History, Dept. of State, Tallahassee
Martha & Stanley Myers, Miami Beach
NASA, Cape Kennedy
Gloria & Leonard Nathanson, Sarasota
National Conference of Christians & Jews, Miami
Sarah Brameister Nelson, Miami
June & E. Charles Oberdorfer, Jacksonville
Orange County Historical Museum, Orlando
Orlando Chevra Kadisha Society, Orlando
Orlando Sentinel, Orlando
Margie Frankel Pariser, Orlando
Pensacola Historical Society, Pensacola
Sylvia Berman Prince, Orlando
Dr. Samuel & Bessie Proctor, Gainesville
Harvey Rifkin, Fort Lauderdale
Riverside Gordon Memorial Chapel, Miami
Dorothy Rombro, Orlando
Sandra & Myron Rosenthal, Pensacola
Susan Rosin, Sarasota
Terry & Dr. Alexander Rosin, Jacksonville
Ruth & Joseph P. Safer, Jacksonville
Tinker Sale, Orlando
Anne Kanner Samuels, Atlanta
Vera & Max Sattler, Melbourne

Nanette Cohen Savage, Miami Beach
Catherine & Rob Schechter, Miami
Vina & William Schemer, Jacksonville
Ann Gundersheimer & Harold Schops, Pensacola
Sylvia Schupler, West Palm Beach
Joan Schwartzman, Miami
Jane G. Seligman, Pensacola
Mardi & Ronald Shader, Orlando
Sylvia & Jack Shorstein, Jacksonville
Brenda Siciliano, Miami
Michael Simonhoff, Miami
Irene & Dr. Roy Sloat, Jacksonville
Shirley Snider, West Palm Beach
Fannie Solomon, Pensacola
Stephen Sonnabend, Key Biscayne
Shirley & Gerald Sonne, Orlando
Mollie Newman Spier, Hallandale
Tibby Burman Spivack, Gainesville
Celia Tanner, Fort Myers
Temple Ahavath Chesed, Jacksonville
Temple Solel, Hollywood
Betty Terry, Orlando
Rose Dubler Toback, Miami
Judith Meitin Toll, Orlando
University of Florida Press, Gainesville
Jackie & Dr. Ervin Wahnish, Orlando
Linda & Paul Wahnish, Annapolis, MD
David Waksman, Miami
Olga Moses Walker, Pompano Beach
Madeleine & Bernie Wall, Miami
Helen Weinfeld, Naples
Barbara Weinstein Company, Miami
Frances & Jack Weintraub, Sarasota
Ruth & Eugene Weiss, Miami
T.T. Wentworth Museum, Pensacola
Lester Wishnatzki, Plant City
Ruth Esther & Joseph Wittenstein, Orlando
Elaine & Richard Wolfson, Miami
Marcia & Elliott Zerivitz, Orlando
Marjorie & Marvin Zuckerman, Miami

EXHIBIT SUPPORTERS

MOSAIC FOUNDERS
($100,000 and more)
Florida Department of State, Tallahassee

QUINCENTENARY CLUB
($50,000 to $99,999)
Historical Museum of Southern Florida, Miami
Judaic Studies Program, University of Miami,
Coral Gables

HERITAGE CLUB
($25,000 to $49,999)
Florida Endowment for the Humanities, Tampa

GUARDIANS OF HISTORY
($10,000 to $24,999)
Maynard & Gertrude Mendelson Abrams,
Delray Beach
Shepard Broad Foundation, Miami
Ruby Diamond Foundation, Tallahassee
Esther & Solomon Garazi, Miami
Evelyn Gross, Boca Raton
Heléne & Bernard Herskowitz, Miami
Sidney W. Langer, Miami
Miami Beach Visitor & Convention Authority
The Miami Herald
Miami Jewish Tribune
Sarasota County Tourist Development Council
Samuel & Helene Soref Jewish Community Center,
Fort Lauderdale
The Ben Stein Family, Jacksonville

BENEFACTORS
($5,000 to $9,999)
Bertha & Leonard Abess, Sr., Miami
Blank Family Foundation, Miami
Dade Community Foundation, Miami
Dr. Ed Dauer, Fort Lauderdale
Children of Albert S. & Ruth Zion Dubbin, Miami
Greater Fort Lauderdale Jewish Federation
The Orovitz Family, Miami
Michael & Norma, Jimmy & Nancy
Richard & Felicia Orovitz Deutch

Betty & Alex Schoenbaum, Sarasota
Helene & Samuel Soref, Fort Lauderdale
Wolfson Family Foundation, Miami

ASSOCIATES
($2,500 to $4,999)
Joanne & Dr. Robert Bass, Miami
Central Agency For Jewish Education,
Miami & Fort Lauderdale
Hazel & Irving Cypen, Miami
Jacksonville Jewish Federation
Pensacola Jewish Federation
Sarasota-Manatee Jewish Federation
Sarasota-Manatee Jewish Foundation
The Kanner Family
Aaron Kanner, Marcia & Lewis Kanner, Miami
Regina & Richard Kanner, Rose & Albert Friedman, Miami
Anne Kanner & Lee Samuel, Atlanta, GA
Cora, Jack, & Murray Kanner, Sanford
Neil & Sandra Angel Malamud & Family, Sarasota
Monsanto Chemical Company, Pensacola
Elizabeth & Edmund Parnes, Miami
Terry & Dr. Alexander Rosin, Jacksonville
Ruth & Sam Seitlin, Miami

SPONSORS
($1,800 to $2,499)
Doris & Bernard G. Blanck, Miami
Roz & Cal Kovens, Miami

DONORS
($1,000 to $1,799)
Samuel Adler Family Foundation, Miami
Ann Broad Bussel, Miami
Ethel & Alvin Cassel, Miami
Israel Consulate, Miami
Spanish Consulate, Miami
Fisher-Brown Insurance, Pensacola
Edgar Galvan, Hollywood
Ganz Family Foundation, Miami
Rose & Leo Gelvan, Miami
Dr. Ruth & Arnold Greenfield
Eleemosynary Fund, Miami
David Wolkowsky, Key West & Edna Wolkowsky, Miami

DONORS
($1,000 to $1,799)
Robbie & Jerome Herskowitz, Miami
Harry Kahn, Pensacola
Beverly & Marvin Kaiman, Pensacola
Karen & Mortimer Kass, Miami
Knight-Ridder, Inc., Miami
Sidney Kohl Foundation, Palm Beach
Kugelman Foundation, Pensacola
Doug Lazarus, Fort Lauderdale
Joan & Dr. Melvin Levinson, Miami
Susan & Bernard S. Ludwig, Miami
Kenneth M. Myers, Miami
Martha S. & Stanley Myers, Miami
Dr. Sidney L. Olson, Miami
W.D. Pollak, Pensacola
Dr. Lawrence Robbins, Miami
Judge Steven Robinson, Miami
Dorothy Rombro, Casselberry
Vera & Max Sattler, Melbourne
Esther & Sidney M. Schwartz, Miami
Sylvia & Jack Shorstein, Jacksonville
Southern Jewish Historical Society
Ted & Rosalind Wedeles Spak, Miami
Mrs. George Terry, Sr., Orlando
Jackie & Robert Traurig, Miami
Uniforms for Industry, Miami
Albert L. Weintraub, Miami
Marjorie & Leonard Wein, Miami
Dr. & Mrs. A.H. Wilkinson, Jr., Jacksonville
Ruth Esther & Joseph Wittenstein, Orlando

PATRONS
($500 to $999)
Annette & David Alpert, Rancho Santa Fe, CA
Anne & David Anchin, Sarasota
Stanley Arkin, Miami
Atico Savings Bank, Miami
Lewis Bear Company, Pensacola
Rosetta & Donald Bierman, Miami
David Catsman, Miami
Jack Coleman, Jacksonville
Sylvia & Dr. Robert Feltman, Miami
Julia Flom, Tampa
Irving & David Gibbs, Orlando
Nancy & Dr. Gerald Goldberg, Fort Lauderdale
Grace & B.B. Goldstein, Miami
Henrietta & James Gordon, Miami
Sarah & Sidney Green, Ottawa, Canada
Nathan & Sophia Gumenick Foundation, Miami
Hallmark Press, Miami

Natalie Glickstein Haas, Jacksonville
Donald P. Kahn, Miami
Helen Kahn, Pensacola
Barbara & Howard Katzen, Miami
Pablo Lapiduz, RudyClar Printing, Miami
Ralph & Bluma Meitin, Orlando
Faith & David Mesnekoff, Miami
E. Charles Oberdorfer, Jacksonville
E. Albert Pallot, Miami
Patricia Meyer & Dr. Emanuel Papper, Miami
Ava & Dr. James Phillips, Fort Lauderdale
Sally & Leonard Robbins, Hollywood
Herschel Rosenthal, Miami
Evelyn & Herman Rubin, Miami
Candace & Lloyd Ruskin, Miami
Dolores & Dr. Kerry Schwartz, Orlando
Bernard & Sheryl Siegel, Miami
Susan Slavin, A Statement in Foods, Miami
Joan & Harry Smith, Miami
Susan & Sam Smith, Miami
Sonnabend Foundation, Miami
Southeast Bank of West Florida, Pensacola
Tampa, Orlando, Pinellas Jewish Foundation, Orlando
Madeleine & Bernard Wall, Miami
Phillip A. Wolff, Sarasota
Richard F. Wolfson, Miami
Marcia & Elliott Zerivitz, Orlando

FRIENDS
($250 to $499)
Albert Cohen, Miami
Karen & Jim Dawkins, Clearwater
Executive Caterers South, Miami
Bruce R. Frank, Miami
Emily Friedman, Miami
Jill & Harold Gaffin, Miami
Gary R. Gerson, Miami
Barbara Seitlin Gillman, Miami
Carol & Morton Goldenblank, Miami
Elizabeth & Henry Green, Miami
Enid Lichter, Sarasota
Barbara Meyer, Miami
Janice Nankin, Fort Lauderdale
Dorothy & Dr. Paul Oberdorfer, Jacksonville
Susan H. Rosin, Sarasota
Ruth & Joseph P. Safer, Jacksonville
Barbara & Benjamin Slavin, Sarasota
Jean & William Soman, Miami
Spector & Sons, Miami
Cindy & Jay Stein, Jacksonville
Carole & Steven Stone, Sarasota

Temple Israel, Tallahassee
Linda & Dr. Howard Zwibel, Miami

CHARTER MEMBERS
($100 to $249)

Laura & Mark Abramson, Orlando
Ellen & Neil Abramson, Jacksonville
Claire Ades, Pensacola
Barbara & Charles Adler, Tampa
Susan B. Albert, Miami
Alpha Omega Dental Fraternity, Miami Chapter
Fran & Dr. Barry Alter, Fort Lauderdale
American Jewish Congress, Florida Chapter, Miami
Gail & Ernest Andich, Miami
Sybil & Lewis Ansbacher, Jacksonville
Dorothy & Arthur Apple, Miami
Marcia & Bernard Applebaum, Miami
Gertrude Arfa, Miami
Aaron Aronson, Jacksonville
Dr. & Mrs. David Aronson, Pensacola
Bonnie Dubbin & Gerald Askowitz, Miami
Clarice & Sam Badanes, Miami
Sandra & Kenneth Baer, Miami
Therese B. & Allan Baer, Fort Lauderdale
Myrna & David Band, Sarasota
Evelyn & Joseph Barbanel, Fort Lauderdale
Gertrude & Marvin Barkin, Tampa
Irene & Bill Baros, Miami
Eunice & Jim Baros, Miami
Ellen & Dr. George Baum, Miami
Louise Srednick Bauer, Miami
Adele S. & Jack Bayer, Miami
Gladys Bear & Family, Sarasota
Millicent Beldner, Miami
Russell E. Belous, Pensacola
Marilyn & Dr. Philip Benjamin, St. Petersburg
Julien P. Benjamin, Jacksonville
Minette Benson, Miami
Helene & Adolph Berger, Miami
Shirley Bergman, Miami
Lisa Medin & Hillel Beriro, Jerusalem, Israel
Florence & Albert Berk, Orlando
Roberta Berkan, Miami
Maureen & Paul Berkowitz, Miami
Sydell & David Berman, Miami
Renée & Marshall Bernard, Miami
Margie & Elihu Bernstein, Tampa
Adele & George Bernstein, Miami
Roslyn & Ray Berrin, Miami
Sylvia Birnbaum, Fort Lauderdale
Rep. Elaine & Judge Philip Bloom, Miami

Jessica Pepper Bloom, Miami
Margery & Mitchell Bloomberg, Miami
Beverlee Boguslaw, Sarasota
Gloria & Ira Boris, Boca Raton
Pola & Ludwik Brodzki, Fort Lauderdale
Judith & Dr. Stuart Brown, Miami
Mildred Weissel Brown, Miami
Barbara & Stanley Bulbin, Miami
Dr. Barry N. Burak, Miami
B'nai Zion Congregation, Key West
Diane & C. Isaac Camber, Miami
Joan & Gary Canner, Miami
Cartaret Bank, Miami
Leslie & Marwin Cassel, Miami
Charlotte Weinkle & Meyer Chazin, Sarasota
Claire & Barnett Chepenik, Orlando
Lois & Alan Chepenik, Jacksonville
Saul Chernowitz, Sarasota
Dora Chutz, Sarasota
Marcia & Philip Cofman, Fort Lauderdale
Esther Neham Cogen, Miami
Burton M. Cohen, Las Vegas, NE
Eleena & David Cohen, Sarasota
Meridith J. "Morty" Cohen, Orlando
Mildred & Phillip Cohen, Fort Lauderdale
Saul S. Cohen, Miami
Sylvia & Gershom Cohn, Sarasota
Mr. & Mrs. Richard Cole, Pensacola
Gertrude & Colson Perry Coleman, Jacksonville
Rosalie & Robert Lee Coleman, Jacksonville
Shirley & Leonard Collman, St. Petersburg
Betty & Marvin Cooper, Miami
Coronet Paper Products, Miami
Maurice Cromer, Miami
Hannah & Maurice Dankoff, Sarasota
Dr. B.V. Dannheisser, Jr., Pensacola
Carol & Dale Davis, Miami
Julius Darsky, Miami
Kathryn W. & Robert S. Davis, Pensacola
Zita & Milford Desenberg, Sarasota
Reva Dessauer, Palm Beach
Flo & Jerry Don, Sarasota
Gladys & Daniel Dubbin, Miami
Janice & Clifford Dubbin, Orlando
Helen & Meyer Eggnatz, Miami
Ann & Link Elozory, Tampa
Selma & Al Emoff, Orlando
Phyllis & Edward Englander, Orlando
Myra & Aaron Farr, Miami
Eva & Steven Feig, Miami
Dr. & Mrs. Fred Felser, Miami

CHARTER MEMBERS
($100 to $249)

Erna Philipson Ferster, Fort Lauderdale
Clara Fine, Miami
Diane & Louis Fine, Miami
Shirley & Abraham Fischler, Hollywood
Adele S. Fischler, Fernandina Beach
Adeline S. Fish, Pensacola
Marsha & Marvin Fish, Pensacola
Kitty & Ernest Fisher, Sarasota
Roberta & Howard Fisher, Miami
Suzanne & Dr. Lawrence Fishman, Miami
Carolyn Wedeles & Arthur Fixel, Quincy
David B. Fleeman, Miami
Ida Engler Forer, Miami
Karen & Richard Forster, Miami
Zetta & Ken Fradin, Sarasota
Jeanne R. Frank, Sarasota
Maxine & Darwin Frank, Clearwater
Ann & Irving Frankel, Miami
Cynthia & Markus Frankel, Miami
Rosalind & Hirsh Freed, Sarasota
Carol & Norman Freedman, Jacksonville
Jules Freeman, Sarasota
Ceresa & Paul Frenkel, Mobile, AL
Lottie Friedland, Fort Lauderdale
Beatrice Friedman, Sarasota
Ben Friedman, Jacksonville
Miriam (Pat) Friedman, Fort Lauderdale
Nellye & Herb Friedman, Tampa
Sabeto Garazi, Miami
Vivian & Rabbi Stanley Garfein, Tallahassee
Phylis & Peter Garvett, Miami
Sylvia & Irving Genet & Donna Genet Loerky, Miami
Martha & Sheldon Gensler, Sarasota
Gladys Gerofsky, Ocala
Mr. & Mrs. David Gibbs, DeLand
Judy Myers Gilbert, Miami
Frances & Norman Giller, Miami
Judge Marvin Gillman, Miami
Laurie & Arthur Ginsburg, Sarasota
Shulamit & Dr. Abraham Gittelson, Miami
Irena & Joel Glaser, Miami
Patricia & Jack Glass, Fort Lauderdale
Gene K. Glasser, Hollywood
Gilda & Martin Glickstein, Jacksonville
Judge Hugh Glickstein, Palm Beach
Alvera Gold, Boca Raton
Rose & Gus Goldenberg, Pensacola
Hedi Goldfarb, Orlando
Roberta M. Golding, Tampa

Mr. & Mrs. Irving Goldberger, Sarasota
Sandra & Max Goldfarb, Miami
Bernice & Jerome Goldman, Sarasota
Mr. & Mrs. Jack Goldsmith, Sarasota
Ann & Alfred Goldstein, Sarasota
Grace Goldstein, Sarasota
Lonnie Golenberg, Fort Lauderdale
Carole Goodman, Boca Raton
Rabbi Ted & Florence Baskin Gordon, Miami
Cheryl & Scott Gordon, Sarasota
Peggy Selig Gordon, Miami
Sylvia R. Gottlieb, Fort Myers
Margo Gould, Fort Lauderdale
Bernice & Samuel Gource, Osprey
Greater Charitable Foundation, Orlando
Nancy Schonfeld Green, Miami
Miriam & Hillel Greenberg, Sarasota
Mildred Greenblatt, Fort Lauderdale
Rabbi Howard Greenstein, Jacksonville
Evelyn R. Gross, Fort Lauderdale
Kathy Ann Gross, Fort Lauderdale
Ruth Frank Gross, Fort Lauderdale
Sarilee & Joel Grossman, Orlando
Sheila & Joel Grossman, St. Petersburg
Sue Anne & Sadie E. Grossman, Miami
Malvina & Dr. Nat Gutschmidt, Miami
Julia & Henry Halpern, Jacksonville
Dr. & Mrs. Lewis Hanan, Sarasota
Dolly & Ernie Harris, Miami
Zelda Harrison, Miami
Lila G. Heatter, Miami
Rose & Larry Hecht, Jacksonville
Rachel Heimovics, Orlando
Helene Curtis Foundation, New York, NY
Patti & Richard Hershorin, Sarasota
Lisa Wolfson Hess, Miami
Mr. & Mrs. Barry Hesser, Miami
Carolyn M. Hirsch, Sarasota
Eileen & Herb Hirsch, Miami
Fred Hirt, Miami
Laura & Richard Hochman, Fort Lauderdale
Jack Hockman, Miami
Deborah & Larry Hoffman, Miami
Alma & Newton Hofstadter, Miami
C. William Homa, Panama Canal Zone
Wendy & Joseph Honigman, Jacksonville
Sonya & Richard Horwich, Miami
Doris & Sam Idelson, Sarasota
Ann C. Jacobs, Fort Lauderdale
Judith & Richard Jacobs, Miami
Lydia & Dr. Jon Jacobs, Fort Lauderdale

Sheila & Leo Jacobson, Jacksonville
Dave & Mary Alper Jewish Community Center, Miami
Jewish Arts Foundation, Palm Beach
Jennie Jones, Sarasota
Albert H. Kahn, Miami
Arthur M. Kahn, Miami
Bettie & Charles Kahn, Pensacola
Carol Andrea Kahn, Pensacola
Janet & Charles Kahn, Jr., Pensacola
H. Dante Kahn, Pensacola
Nathan A. Kahn, Pensacola
Mr. & Mrs. H. Dante Kahn, Jr., Pensacola
Natalie & Jay Kaiman, Pensacola
Edward Kalin, Sarasota
Phyllis & Abe Kamenoff, Orlando
Anne & Bernard Kantor, Tampa
Barbara Kanzer, Miami
Betsy Kaplan, Miami
Estelle & Harry Kaplan, Melbourne
Helen Kaplan, Miami
Jerome Kapner, Sarasota
Jeanette & Ben Karasick, Sarasota
Carolyn & Stephen Kass, Fort Lauderdale
Bunny & Abe Katz, St. Petersburg
Gail & Dr. Bernard Katz, Sarasota
Carole & Ronald Katz, Jacksonville
Henrietta & Marc Katzen, Orlando
Clara Kaufman, Fort Lauderdale
Irma & Simon Kaufman, Sarasota
Josephine W. Kenin, Miami
Edythe & Elton Kerness, Miami
Shirley Kerze, Orlando
Martha & Ben Klein, Miami
Ida Koenigsberg, St. Petersburg
Elaine & William Kopans, Sarasota
Mr. Koslow, Fort Lauderdale
Helen & Meyer Kotler, Miami
Kathy & James Kramer, Miami
Heather & Stephen Kravitz, Miami
Mr. & Mrs. Richard Kronenberg, Miami
Dr. Stephen Kulvin, Miami
Suetelle & Alan Kurzweil, Miami
Roberta & Dr. Miles Kuttler, Miami
Harriett & Hymen Lake, Orlando
Dr. Sol Landau, Miami
Sophie & Isidore Landsman, Fort Lauderdale
Karen & Dr. Robert Lavine, Pensacola
Maye & Sherman Lavinson, Sarasota
Florence Lebos, Tampa
Joan & Congressman Bill Lehman, Miami
Marjorie & Paul Lehrer, Miami

Dr. Irving Lehrman, Temple EmanuEl, Miami
Myrna Leonard, Miami
Hope & Joel C. Leuchter, Sarasota
Abe Levin, Pensacola
Fredric G. Levin, Pensacola
Claire & Richard Levin, Sarasota
Hildreth Levin, Fort Lauderdale
Susana G. & Jack H. Levine, Miami
Gloria & Saul Levinson, Sarasota
Dorothy & Sol Levites, Sarasota
Rhoda Levitt, Miami
Bonnie Cohn Levy, Orlando
Marie B. & Dick Levy, Fort Lauderdale
Elvire & Lucien Levy, Sarasota
George A. Levy, Tampa
Patricia & Leonard Levy, Tampa
Alice & Sam Lewinson, Fort Lauderdale
Patricia & Warren Lieberman, Miami
Marilyn & Y. Stephen Liedman, Miami
Ann Spector Leiff, Miami
Bea & Irving Lippton, Orlando
May & Frank Lipschutz, Miami
Dava & Michael Lipsky, Miami
Doris Loevner, Sarasota
Phyllis & Julius Lovitz, Clearwater
Anna Ludwig, Miami
Suzanne & David Lutkoff, Sarasota
Natalie Lyons, Miami
Mr. & Mrs. J.L. Mack, Jr., Jacksonville
Dr. Robert Magoon, Miami
Sonia & Lester Mandell, Orlando
Ellen & Bernard Mandler, Miami
Pat & Hal Marcus, Pensacola
Florence Markowitz, Miami
Patricia & Robert Markowitz, Miami
Harriet & Edwin Masinter, Palm Beach
Rita & Barry Mazer, Sarasota
Robert McPherson, Orlando
Debbie & Samuel Meitin, Orlando
Norman Mendelson, Fort Lauderdale
Sidney W. Mendelson, Tallahassee
Max Merdinger, Sarasota
Evelyn Kanner Merkin & Family, Atlanta, GA
Charlyne & Jim Meyer, Miami
Greater Miami Foundation of Jewish Philanthropies
Art Michaels, Sarasota
Estelle & Bernard Michelson, Miami
Marian & Marc Milgram, Miami
Sonya & Irwin Miller, St. Petersburg
Phyllis & Harvey Miller, Miami
James Fox Miller, Hollywood

CHARTER MEMBERS
($100 to $249)
Sylvia & Sandford Milter, Sarasota
Karl Mindlin, Miami
Belle & Lee Mintz, Sarasota
Hortense & Joseph Mintzer, Sarasota
Larry Mizrach, Miami
Mildred Morganstern, Fort Lauderdale
Marlene & Lester Morris, Orlando
Morse Geriatric, Palm Beach
Ethel & Isadore Moscovitz, Jacksonville
Raela & Norman Moss, Jacksonville
Ethel & Donald Murray, Miami
Marlene & Wayne Myers, Jacksonville
Gloria & Leonard Nathanson, Sarasota
Sarah & Theodore Nelson, Miami
Joyce & Justin Oppenheim, Palm Beach
Claire Ordon, Pensacola
Nedra & Dr. Mark Oren, Miami
Ruth R. Orne, Sarasota
Ethel C. Ornstein, Sarasota
Esta & Robert Orovitz, Miami
Gloria & Norton Pallot, Miami
Gloria & Ronald Pallot, Miami
Joseph Wedeles Pallot, Miami
Melissa Aden Pallot, Miami
William Pallot, Miami
Papertree & Estabelle, Miami
Ida Pasternak, Fort Lauderdale
Nancy & Edward Pastroff, Miami
Doris & Paul Paver, Sarasota
Abraham Peck, American Jewish Archives, Cincinnati, OH
Rita & David Perlman, Miami
Beatrice & Irving Peskoe, Homestead
Sam Pinsky, Orlando
Mollie Pollack, Fort Lauderdale
Lucille & Nathan Poller, Tampa
Marsha & Ronnie Pollock, Jacksonville
Sydney Pomer, Sarasota
Don Pravda, Miami
Rhoda Pritzer, Sarasota
Irving Proctor, Jacksonville
Dr. & Mrs. Samuel Proctor, Gainesville
Rochelle & Sol Proctor, Jacksonville
Lois & Dr. Ira Rashkin, Sarasota
Pearl & Joel Reinstein Philanthropic Fund, Fort Lauderdale
Sheila & Dr. Sorrel Resnik, Miami
Nan & David Rich, Miami
Greta & Nat Rickoff, Pensacola
Honey-Miam Robbins, Miami

Shirley & Norman Robbins, Orlando
Ellen & Steve Rose, Hollywood
Muriel & Arnold Rosen, Miami
Robert Rosen, Miami
Faye & Joe Rosenbaum, Pensacola
Sharon & Gene Rosenbaum, Pensacola
Claire Becker & Jack Rosenberg, Orlando
Doris & Frank L. Rosenblatt, Tampa
Linda & Dr. Robert Rosenbluth, Sarasota
Lois & Jerome C. Rosenthal, Sarasota
Sandra & Myron Rosenthal, Pensacola
Mack Roth, Daytona Beach
Sharon & Martin Rothberg, Miami
Elaine & Harvey Rothenberg, Sarasota
Nancy & Jerry Roucher, Sarasota
Irene & Paul Rubenstein, Tampa
Lois & Edward S. Rubin, Miami
Lisa & Jon Rubenstein, Sarasota
Miriam Sager Saffer, Miami
Marjorie Sagman, Sarasota
Muriel & Morris Salomon, Miami
Minnie C. Salsbury, Tampa
Norma Salz, Miami
Susan & Dr. Russell Samson, Sarasota
Jeff Saster, Fort Lauderdale
Madelyn Saul, Miami
Nanette Cohen Savage, Miami
Gloria G. & Howard Scharlin, Miami
Catherine & Roy Schechter, Jr., Miami
Margrit & Jerome Schechtman, Sarasota
Dr. Peritz Scheinberg, Miami
Schemer-Slott Reunion, Jacksonville
Stanley Schmerken, Pensacola
Ann & Harold Schops, Pensacola
Thelma & Sol Schreiber, Miami
Lynne Schulte, Miami
Bernese Schwartz, Miami
Charlotte & Leon Schwartz, Tampa
Melissa & Philip Schwartz, Miami
Ruth & Irving Schwartz, Miami
Sonia & Amb. William Schwartz, Sarasota
Estelle & Ira Segal, Miami
Teddi B. & Norton Segal, Miami
Hilda & Dr. David Seitlin, Miami
Mary & Leonard Selber, Jacksonville
Philip Selber, Jacksonville
Selevan Family Foundation, Jacksonville
Lillian & Abe Senser, Sarasota
Ruth & Richard Shack, Miami
Mark Shader, Orlando
Shader Investment Company, Orlando

Rabbi Howard Shapiro, Palm Beach
Carol & Murray Shear, Miami
Anna & Marvin Sheldon, Miami
Rita & Frank Shewer, Sarasota
Gerd & Muriel Shindler, Sarasota
Audrey Maas & Mark Shine, Tampa
Suzanne & Fred K. Shochet, Miami
Cecelia Wahnish Shopiro, Miami
Rabbi Albert & Rose Shulman, Sarasota
Golda & Robert Siegel, Miami
Helene & Judge Sam Silver, Miami
Beverly & Sheldon Silverstein, Sarasota
Herbert Silverstein, Sarasota
Julie & Gary Simon, Miami
Ilse Simonhoff, Miami
Ned F. Sinder, Miami
Lee Sinoff, Miami
Edward Sirkin, Miami
Dr. & Mrs. Laurence Skolnik, Fort Lauderdale
Dr. & Mrs. Roy Julius Sloat, Jacksonville
Jeanie & Harvey Small, Sarasota
Mrs. Morris Soble, Chicago, IL
Marilyn & Joseph Solomon, Miami
Erica & David Sommer, Miami
Melvyne Wahnish Sommers, Miami
Steven Sommers, Houston, TX
Shirley & Gerald Sonne, Orlando
Shirley & Bill Spear, Miami
Simeon Spear, Miami
Melba & Jack Speckert, Miami
Heather & Ron Spector, Sarasota
Ruth Spector, Miami
Corinne Speer, Pensacola
Barry J. Spiegel, Miami
Mollie Newman Spier, Fort Lauderdale
Linda Morrell & Dr. Norman Spitzer, Miami
Marjorie Spritzer, Miami
Dorothy & David Stevens, Sarasota
Richard & Marlene Stone, Washington, DC
Florence Strauss, Fort Lauderdale
Linda & Jeffrey Streitfeld, Fort Lauderdale
Rosalyn & Charles Stutzin, Miami
Betty & Cliff Suchman, Miami
Rita & Bernard Switchkow, Miami
Romelle & Nathan Tarler, Fort Lauderdale
Stanley Tate, Miami
Mr. & Mrs. Jack Taylor, Miami
Judi & Philip Taylor, Miami
Charlton Tebeau, Springfield, GA
Temple Beth Shalom Sisterhood, Sarasota
Temple Emanu-El, Sarasota

Temple Israel, Palm Beach
Temple Israel Sisterhood, Daytona Beach
Temple Kol Ami, Plantation
Temple Shalom, Naples
Temple Shir Shalom, Gainesville
Melanie Thurman, Miami
Roberta & D. Stephen Toback, Miami
Judith Meitin Toll, Orlando
Florence Tobias, Orlando
Adrienne & Richard Tufeld, Studio City, CA
Susan & Stephen Turner, Tallahassee
Caryl Rose & Dr. Harold Unger, Miami
Esther L. Van Tuin, Sarasota
Mr. & Mrs. George Wagenheim, Pensacola
Jacqueline & Dr. Ervin Wahnish, Orlando
Edna & David Warsowe, Fort Lauderdale
Lawrence Wartell, Orlando
Hannah Wartenberg, Miami
Sherry & Dr. Daniel Watts, Sarasota
Raquel & Stanley Wax, Miami
Ruth & Dr. William Waxman, Orlando
Malka & Neil Webman, Orlando
Naomi Meitin & Dr. Harold Webman, Miami
Bella Kudisch Weinberg, Sarasota
Gwen & Morton Weinberger, Miami
Jane L. & Robert H. Weiner, Fort Lauderdale
Frances & Jack Weintraub, Sarasota
Richard Weintraub, Sarasota
Helen Weisberg, Miami
Ruth & Eugene Weiss, Miami
Marilyn & Irving Weissman, Tampa
Barbara & Michael Weitz, Miami
Marcella Unger Werblow, Miami
Theresa & Joseph Wertheimer, Sarasota
Mr. & Mrs. Marvin Wiener, Miami
Sally & Earl Wiener, Miami
Gertrude & Lionel Willins, Sarasota
Wishnatzki & Nathel, Plant City
Jessie & Bernard Wolfson, Miami
Paul Reinholz Quitman Wolfson, Miami
Madeline & George Wolly, Orlando
Frances & David Yelen, Miami
Bobbi Yoffe, Jacksonville
Barbara Hirsch York, Sarasota
Miriam & Milton Zatinsky, Miami
Paula & Dr. Carl Zielonka, Tampa
Sylvia & Ewald Ziffer, Miami
Ada Zimmerman, Fort Lauderdale
Bill, Beverly, Benjamin, Joshua Zimmern, Pensacola
Eve W. Zinner, Miami
Gertrude G. Zion, Miami

CHARTER MEMBERS
($100 to $249)
Arline & Matthew Zucker, Miami
Marjorie & Marvin Zuckerman, Miami

CONTRIBUTORS
(under $100)
Ruth & Moe Aronson, Orlando
Marvin Aronovitz, Tampa
Michelle Pivar & Jack Barr, Miami
Jack Becker, Jacksonville
Lois & Max Bender, Miami
Diane & David Berman, Orlando
Jill & Leonard Bloom, Miami
Ann Bosch, Miami
Brandeis Women, Fort Lauderdale
Mascha Braun, Sarasota
Iris & Ben Bush, St. Petersburg
Vonda & Orville Clayton, Sarasota
Sylvia & Aaron Cohen, Miami
William B. Cooper, Miami
Shirley & Oscar Dinkin, Sarasota
Joan & Jerry Esrick, St. Petersburg
Judah Evers, Fort Lauderdale
Carole & William Foor, Miami
Patricia & Myer Frank, Tampa
Mary & Steven Friedman, Miami
Henry Gillman, Miami
Marilyn Mittentag & Stuart Gitlitz, Miami
Julia Goldstein, Tallahassee
Minerva Goldstein, Sarasota
Rabbi Paul Grob, Satellite Beach
Palm Beach Jewish Community Center
Michael Ann Russell, Jewish Community Center, Miami
Palm Beach Jewish Day School
Palm Beach Jewish Family & Childrens Services
Judy & Robert Hara, Orlando
Men's Club of Hi Greens, Fort Lauderdale
Abraham D. Horn, Sarasota

Wayne M. Hosid, Tallahassee
Joyce Dorothy Korn, Tallahassee
Rabbi Sidney & Mrs. Lefkowitz, Jacksonville
Lois & Michael Legg, Orlando
Charna Lester, St. Petersburg
Barbara Levy, Miami
Rosalind & Isadore Levy, Miami
Gail S. Meyers, Miami
Belle & Lee Mintz, St. Petersburg
Adele Morris, St. Petersburg
Museum of the Southern Jewish
Experience, Jackson, MS
New World School of the Arts, Miami
Edith & Stuart Newman, Miami
Judge Robert & Gail Newman, Miami
Carol & Irvin Peckett, Tampa
Sylvia & Ernest Rapp, Orlando
Rabbi & Mrs. A.E. Resnicoff, Pensacola
Mildred & Jack Ross, Fort Lauderdale
Ethel Rothenberg, Orlando
Renee & Larry Salzer, St. Petersburg
Ruth K. Silverman, Sarasota
Alexander Siskind Family Trust, Orlando
Zelda & Melvin Siskind, Sanford
Leon Sobel, Orlando
Tybel Spivack, Gainesville
Cornelia & Melvin Stein, Tampa
Robert S. Steinberg, Miami
Lucille Strauss, St. Petersburg
Abraham Sweedler, Orlando
Temple Beth Israel, Sanford
Temple Beth Israel Sisterhood, Fort Lauderdale
Temple Israel, Miami
Mrs. Oscar Thaler, Fort Lauderdale
Dorothy & Harry Verstandig, Jacksonville
Womens American ORT, Fort Lauderdale
Ruth Wormser, St. Petersberg
Rosalind & Jack Zacks, Miami